"Precious few marriage coaches know how to connect with couples the way Bill and Pam Farrel do. They are always delightful guests on my program with great stories that illustrate biblical marriage in a fun and entertaining manner. Lots of us, thanks to them, will now be unlocking the secrets of *The Marriage Code*."

—**FRANK PASTORE,** host of *The Frank Pastore Show*

"Bill and Pam Farrel are gifted speakers who effectively communicate marriage principles that work. They skillfully weave biblical truth with practical tools that assist couples in understanding how to decode each other's basic needs. The end result is staying power, contentment, and joy. I highly recommend *The Marriage Code* and study guide."

—**CAROL KENT,** author of *A New Kind of Normal*

"Bill and Pam Farrel are two highly regarded Christian marriage experts. Their writing is right on target and is exactly what the doctor ordered. Bill and Pam's teaching is practical, engaging, and served with a sweet slice of humor. And not only do they talk the talk, they live out what they write and teach. Couples will be blessed by spending time with *The Marriage Code*. It will change their marriage and their life."

—**MITCH TEMPLE,** marriage and family therapist
and author of *The Marriage Turnaround*

THE
MARRIAGE
CODE

BILL & PAM
FARREL

HARVEST HOUSE PUBLISHERS

EUGENE, OREGON

Published in association with the literary agency of Alive Communications, Inc., 7680 Goddard Street,
Ste #200, Colorado Springs, CO 80920. www.alivecommunications.com.

Cover design by Left Coast Design, Portland, Oregon.

Cover photo © Mark Evans/iStockphoto

The Marriage Code
Copyright © 2009 by Bill and Pam Farrel
Published by Harvest House Publishers
Eugene, Oregon 97402
www.harvesthousepublishers.com

Library of Congress Cataloging-in-Publication Data
    Farrel, Bill, 1959-
    The marriage code / Bill and Pam Farrel.
        p. cm.
    ISBN 978-0-7369-1641-7 (pbk.)
    1. Marriage—Religious aspects—Christianity. 2. Interpersonal communication—Religious
aspects—Christianity. I. Farrel, Pam, 1959-
    II. Title.
    BV835.F37 2008
    248.8'44—dc22
                                                                    2008002128

09 10 11 12 13 14 15 16 / DP-SK / 10 9 8 7 6 5 4 3 2 1

Contents

To Bret and Erin
Happy 25th!
Your love is inspiring!

To our friends, family, and supportive staff,
Your love is essential!

To our editorial team and publisher,
Your love is encouraging!

To our readers,
Your love is a light!

Chapter 1

In Search of the Marriage Code

We checked into the hotel and were pleased to see that the room included free wireless Internet. We needed to check our e-mail for some timely travel information and for a message from the office that affected the meeting we were about to attend. When we got to the room, we discovered that we needed a username and password to get to the free wireless connection.

"Hello, this is Bill in 213. Can I get the username and password for the Internet?"

"Shuh [sure], sir. It very simple," the desk clerk said.

I knew right away we were in trouble. Any time you have to say, "It is simple," you really mean, "You are about to be very frustrated."

I pulled out a piece of paper and got my pen ready. "Okay, what is the username?"

"It is barebe," the man said.

"Barebe? Can you spell that?"

"Shuh, it is simple. Capitow Bee–ee–err–i–ee–bee–ee."

"Was that Beriebe?" I asked.

"Oh, no. That not it. It is capitow bee–ee–err–i–ee–bee–ee."

He acted as if he had actually said something different. I guess it was different since his voice was slower and louder this time, but it sounded like the same letters.

"So it is Beriebe?"

"Oh, no. I am sorry. Let's try again."

"Let's try the password and then come back to the username," I said, hoping I could train myself to decipher his language. "So, what is the password?"

"Okay. The password. That is easy. The password is freerarrey-free."

"Can you spell that for me?"

"Shuh, that is easy. Free–arr–aa–err–err–ee–y–free."

"I'll be right down," I said.

I made my way down to the front desk. The man working the counter was very helpful, even though we were having trouble communicating. He wrote down the information for me so I could finally log in and get to the information I needed:

Username: Believe

Password: 3ralley3

What Did You Say?

Has it ever felt the same way in your marriage? You long for emotional, relational, spiritual, and physical connection. You had hoped it would feel as simple as it did when you first started dating or when you were on your honeymoon. Instead of being able to read your mate's thoughts, feelings, and moods, you keep running into an "error" when you try to log in to his or her heart. In place of a heart-to heart-connection, you get a message that reads:

Task "mail.understandingyourmate.com—sending" reported error (UrOutUvLuk): "The operation timed out trying to decipher a message from the sending (MATE) server. If you continue to receive this message, install your personal version of The Marriage Code and resend the message."

Codes Are All Around Us

It is possible to have a marriage that is smooth and satisfying, but you have to know and use the access code that keeps the connection to your spouse alive and well. Codes are all around us. We have access codes for gates and bank accounts. We have passwords for personal computers, professional workstations, and interactive websites. We have remote controls for our cars, televisions, and home theatre systems. And we are captivated with entertainment that depicts investigators who seek to decode the mysteries of life. We have actually found a way to make the tedious work of forensics, crime scene investigation, and the diagnosing of illnesses seem like a fun, recreational activity.

> It is possible to have a marriage that is smooth and satisfying, but you have to know and use the access code that keeps the connection to your spouse alive and well.

We gain directions from Global Positioning Systems, we see bar codes on everything we buy, and we have become comfortable with credit cards that contain vital information on magnetic strips. The military uses codes to keep our nation safe. Businesses use codes to track clients, forecast buying patterns, and safeguard professional intelligence.

Codes come in all shapes and sizes and can be very useful in helping us gain confidence and information. However, the decoding process is not always easy.

Houston, We Have a Problem

The need for codes is clearly displayed in our interaction with computer technology. If you give your computer directions it understands, it will perform for you and enhance your life. If, however, you interact with it contrary to its design, you will end up frustrated, wondering why you ever got involved in the first place. Fortunately, technical help is available if you are willing to pursue it. I (Pam) don't know about you, but I am forever grateful for computer technicians. I need their assistance periodically, but I hope I don't sound like some of their worst nightmare clients. I have to admit, though, that at times I've felt like this poor chap who called in for tech support:

Tech Support: "I need you to right click on the Open Desktop."

Customer: "OK."

Tech Support: "Did you get a pop-up menu?"

Customer: "No."

Tech Support: "OK. Right click again. Do you see a pop-up menu?"

Customer: "No."

Tech Support: "OK, sir. Can you tell me what you have done up until this point?"

Customer: "Sure, you told me to write *click* and I wrote *click*."

(At this point I had to put the caller on hold to tell the rest of the tech support staff what had happened. I couldn't, however, stop from giggling when I got back to the call.)

Tech Support: "OK, did you type *click* with the keyboard?"

Customer: "I've done something dumb, right?"[1]

The Difference Maker

I (Pam) recently upgraded to a new computer, and I must have accidentally hit a wrong button because all the codes that tell a computer what to do were appearing in the text. Knowing I couldn't send a letter that looked like that, I grabbed my laptop and headed for Bill's office.

He was in the middle of a relationship coaching session with Steve and Beth, but he could read the distress on my face and graciously invited me in and introduced me to the couple. I then, very emotionally, pleaded for help. Bill couldn't figure out what I had done or how to undo it either, which made me feel like I wasn't as dumb as I was thinking I was.

Then Beth said, "Would you like me to try? I'm a programmer." After one mouse click, she fixed the issue and told me how to fix it in the future. Then she said, "I have the training that helps me understand computer codes. You both have the training to help us in relationship codes. Knowing the code makes all the difference."

You Have a Code

So, what is "the marriage code"? It is a combination of usernames and passwords that grant you access to the best parts of your relationship. When these codes are in place, your relationship appears to be relatively easy. The way you interact, love, argue, and make decisions is satisfying for you as a couple. When the code is missing, all the systems of your relationship are awkward. You fail in your attempts to connect emotionally, your love for each other is elusive, and you seem to disagree on just about everything.

The following are important truths you need to know about your marriage code:

- It is obvious when the code is in place because your relationship works well.

- It is just as obvious when the code is *not* in place because almost everything is out of sync.

- Entering the marriage code into your relationship is a daily exercise. In the same way that you need to enter a username and password into your computer each time you start it up, your love relationship needs an access code every day.

- The marriage code is based on the most common needs that men and women have.

You may be asking, "Why do we need a code to figure each other out? Can't it just be simple? Can't we discover a rhythm for our relationship and stay in that rhythm?" We hate to have to say to you that it is just not that simplistic. You are very different from one another, and you have different needs at the core of who you are. These needs shape the way you approach life and the way you interact in relationships.

So, just what are these core needs? Every person has the need to be secure and to be successful. *Security* is the belief that it is safe to be who I am. Somewhere along the path of your life, you come to the realization that you have only so much control over your life. You have been given a personality that determines your preferences and motivations. You have been created either male or female with all the hormonal, emotional, and social challenges that go along with your gender. You have a certain level of intellectual prowess and talents that you can apply to your life. Finally, you have a body that is remarkable in its abilities but vulnerable to your environment. As a result, you must devote energy in your life to developing and maintaining a secure environment for yourself and your loved ones.

Success is the belief that my life is workable. I can do what is required of me in the pursuits and responsibilities that I have committed to. It includes having a productive career and making enough money for the family, but it is not limited to this. Your sense of success will also encompass the way you interact with each other, raise your children, take care of your body, cope with stress, make decisions, and manage your time. It will also be expressed in your sense of purpose. You may not be able to clearly state your purpose, but you have a sense of whether your life matters, and you like life better when it feels like it matters.

The Balancing Act

As a single person, you were probably good at keeping these needs in balance. Since you could make all the decisions for your life, you were free to develop just how much you wanted to focus on security and how much you wanted to focus on success. During your dating years, it was probably also relatively simple to maintain the balance you are most comfortable with because you could always go back to your home at the end of the day. Even if you encountered rough times, you would naturally take a break from one another, reestablish your equilibrium as an individual, and then get back together again.

Then you decided to get married. As a couple, you have probably discovered that you approach security and success differently.

The Quest for Security

For most women, security is a more vibrant and common need than success. It isn't that we don't want to succeed; it is simply that we view success as a means for providing security. The need to feel secure is the need we feel most often, and it determines the quality of every-thing in our lives. Security is often difficult for men to understand because it is all consuming in our lives, and it changes faces quickly. Security in our lives includes:

- Physical safety
- Having enough money to meet our family's needs
- Being valued by the people we love the most
- Having opportunities to express ourselves and our convictions
- Having opportunities to be productive
- Having a place to call home
- Having time to take care of ourselves
- Being pampered every once in a while
- Knowing that my husband cares about the things that are important to me
- The freedom to be who I am today

Without a doubt, the last statement, "the freedom to be who I am today," is at the heart of what it means to be secure. As women, our lives are constantly changing. It begins with the "gift" of menstruation. This lovely part of our lives guarantees that our emotions, our bodies, and our outlook on life are in constant motion. Some days we feel great about ourselves and are ready to face any challenge. On other days, we feel bloated and ugly and worthless. Still other days find us sad, anxious, and overreacting. And these days come and go every month! As a result, we are very "interesting" to live with. You might have clues your wife is struggling with PMS when:

- She stops reading *Glamour* and starts reading *Guns and Ammo*.
- She considers chocolate a major food group.
- She retains more water than Lake Superior.
- She denies she's in a bad mood as she pops a clip into her semiautomatic and chambers one.
- She buys you a new T-shirt with a bull's-eye on the front.

- You ask her to please pass the salt at the dinner table, and she says, "All I ever do is give, give, give! AM I SUPPOSED TO DO EVERYTHING?"
- She enrolls in the Lizzie Borden School of Charm.
- She orders three Big Macs, four large fries, a bucket of Chicken McNuggets, and then screams at the manager because they're out of Diet Coke.

In our hearts, we long to find someone who will accept us and love us through the good days and bad days that happen so close to each other. We carry a silent fear that our emotional swings will eventually drive away our husbands, which make this need even more sensitive. As a result, we often react to our spouses with either outbursts or silence. Our reactions tend to be so strong that our husbands actually think we are confident about what we are doing.

This misinterpreted confidence most often shows up in conversation. It has been proven that we women can sense when something is wrong in the important relationships in our lives. When the realization hits us, we begin to bring up the issues. We may not know exactly what the issue is; we just know there is one. Our poor husbands think we know what the issue is because we approach the conversation with such intensity. We don't want to admit that we are searching because that will make us feel incompetent and insecure. We may even be aware that we are being unreasonable, but we continue with the hope that he can handle us.

Bill and I were sitting at my computer working on a project together. I didn't know why, but I was upset with him. Everything he said to me was irritating. His ideas felt like controlling statements. I felt a strange resistance in my heart to everything he wanted to do. Bill tried numerous times to break through, to no avail.

In frustration, he finally blurted out, "Wow, you really miss me, don't you?"

It was as if a plug was pulled and all the frustration drained out of me. He had nailed my emotional need for security right on the head.

His schedule had been so hectic during that time of our life, I began to wonder if he thought I was more important than his work and if I would ever have his full attention again. Just having him notice my pain was enough to release it. I immediately relaxed in my chair, smiled at Bill, and sheepishly said, "Yes. Could you tell?" Of course he could tell. He had just pointed it out, but I wanted to hear him say it.

His acceptance and compassion for who I was changed the environment of the rest of the day. It was one of those days for me as a woman when things look overwhelming, and I needed to hear that I was secure with Bill. I still battled frustration all day, but we faced it together rather than me taking it out on Bill.

The Journey to Success

For most men, success is a more vibrant and common need than security. It's not that we don't want to be secure; it is simply that we will sacrifice security in order to do what we are best at. The need to feel successful is the need we feel most often, and it determines the quality of everything in our lives. A man's approach to success is often confusing to women because it isn't always about being productive. It is about spending our time, money, and energy on the areas of life we know we are good at. We are highly motivated to focus on these areas. At the same time, we are intensely disinterested in the areas of life we don't think we are good at. Success in our lives, therefore, includes:

- Discovering what we do well and what we don't do well
- Spending time doing what we do well
- Evaluating our lives based on what we do well
- Making a fierce commitment to doing what we do well
- Hoping for relationships that work
- Avoiding the areas of life that don't work
- Wanting to spend the majority of our time at things we get complimented on

- Desiring to make relationships as simple as possible to insure success
- Wanting life to feel smooth and easy because we are competent at the majority of the tasks asked of us

The most comprehensive statement that describes a man's need for success is that he will make a "fierce commitment to doing what he does well." Most of us understand this when a man commits to being productive. If he is busy at work, busy at coaching his children's sports teams, busy maintaining the house, the yard, and the car, we admire him. We know that many men can become obsessed with these pursuits and neglect those he cares about, but it seems like a natural struggle.

It is a little more confusing when a man decides to succeed at being an underachiever. These primary needs—security and success—are self-defined so that success means one thing to one man and another to another man. A man who is consistently criticized, especially during his childhood, may conclude that he is good at being lazy or less than competent. If the conclusion sets in, he will fiercely commit to being an underachiever. You can point out his shortcomings, challenge him to action, and point out how he can succeed, and he will still underachieve because he believes this is what he is best at.

It is common for a man to be highly productive in some areas of life while he lacks confidence in other areas. It affects the marriage relationship in that he will put a lot of effort into the areas he is proficient in while he tries to avoid the challenging areas. This is a struggle because he probably feels deficient in the areas his wife is strongest in.

For instance, a common request we hear from wives is, "I wish my husband would talk with me more." Or "How do I get my husband to open up to me?" Compared to their wives, most husbands feel they are behind the game when it comes to conversation. She talks faster than he does, changes subjects faster than he can track, and she gains energy from the discussion. He feels behind from the beginning as he tries to figure out the conversation. Everything he says is like a switch that gives his wife more to talk about. When the conversation is over, he is probably tired. Over time, he concludes this is not a strength of his, so he begins to avoid discussion in favor of activities that make him feel successful.

The marriage code, therefore, is counterintuitive. The username and password that will give a man access to a workable relationship with his wife is:

Username: *Husband*

Password: *Security*

The password that men would prefer to enter is *success*. He is comfortable with this approach to life, and he longs for it to be true. His greatest desire is to help his wife succeed at what she wants to do in life.

- When she talks about a problem she's facing, he wants to solve the problem for her and be her hero.

- When he senses she is frustrated with her life, he concludes that she would do better if she got a job and started being more productive.

- He wants to have simple conversations with straightforward decisions.

- He wants to give her advice about how to control her emotions, stick with commitments, and be level headed.

He has no idea that these messages all make her feel insecure in the relationship because she cannot be who she really is. Instead, she feels as though she has to put on an act around her husband to be who he wants her to be. She knows in her soul that this is not how relationships are supposed to be, so she becomes argumentative or stubborn.

The marriage code goes active when a man learns to enter *security* as the password. He does this when he makes it his ambition to meet his wife's security need first in all things. Any time she gets the message from him, "You are safe with me, and it is all right to be who you are right now," her heart is drawn toward him and she relaxes in the relationship.

It is a learned skill for men because it goes against our instincts.

The username and password that will give a woman access to a secure relationship with her husband is:

Username: *Wife*

Password: *Success*

The password that women would prefer to enter is *security*. She is comfortable with this approach to life, and she longs for it to be true. Her greatest desire is to connect to her husband emotionally, socially, recreationally, spiritually, and financially. She wants to explore the relationship and help her husband experience the emotional fullness she lives with.

- When they talk, she wants to share an emotional connection with her husband.

- She wants her husband to care about life like she cares about life.

- When he is frustrated with his life, she assumes he will be better if he talks about it.

- She wants to give him advice about how to make better decisions, relate to people better, and develop better habits.

This is all sincerely motivated, but it makes him feel controlled rather than respected. He begins to conclude that he can never do enough or can't do what he does well enough to please her. Conversations that used to be enjoyable now turn defensive.

The marriage code goes active when women learn to enter *success* as the password. She does this when she makes it her ambition to create an environment where her husband can succeed with her. Any time he gets the message from her, "I love the way you live and I love the way you love me," his heart is drawn toward her, and he gains confidence in the relationship.

It also is a learned skill for women because it goes against our instincts. Men will conclude the relationship is working when he sees the following:

- Spending time with his wife lowers the stress level in his life
- They make decisions and stick to the decisions
- There is laughter when he spends time with his wife
- He has time to work on his commitments
- His wife continues to flirt with him
- His efforts to build the relationship are greeted with compliments

The Learning Curve

We were almost totally unaware of the marriage code when we first got married. Pam was so easy to be around when we were dating that I thought she would be the easiest person to live with that I had ever met. She was full of energy, laughed every day, and had a simple dedication to helping others grow and learn more about Jesus. I would never have guessed that insecurity could interrupt her day and challenge my confidence in our relationship.

Bill was so calm and flexible with changes and so dedicated to Jesus that I figured it would be simple to live with him. I honestly believed he would adjust to any emotional swings in my life, he would roll with any challenges that presented themselves, and he would remain steady during any stressors we faced. I never would have guessed that his need to succeed could make him stubborn and distant.

I (Bill) remember when I first became aware of the intensity of Pam's need for security. It surfaced during our honeymoon. We escaped to a mountain resort for a week to get intimately acquainted with each other. She was critical of herself every day. She wasn't tall enough, her skin wasn't smooth enough, her hair was too curly, her voice was too high pitched, and on and on. I found myself doing more reassuring of her than anyone I had ever spent time with. I was glad to do it, but I certainly did not see it coming ahead of time.

At the end of the week we traveled to Idaho to stay with her mom for a few days and attend a reception in our honor with her family and friends. During our visit, Pam was being difficult and bossy, so her siblings began to tease her. It looked to me like the simple kind of interaction that brothers and sisters get into, but Pam got her feelings hurt. I got caught up in the teasing and began to laugh, which made Pam even more upset. She shot me a look that sent shivers up my spine and stormed off to our bedroom. It didn't take an advanced degree to realize that something was wrong, so I followed her.

"Pam, what is wrong?"

"You took their side. I am your wife, and you took their side!"

I didn't even realize there were sides to take in this situation. It was a casual conversation, and I am pretty sure Pam had been teased by her brother and sister before. They were not trying to defeat her; they were simply trying to figure out how to have an older sister who was now married. Apparently, I was supposed to jump up from my seat and say to her brother and sister, "I will never allow you to ever be mean to Pam again. I am her husband, and I am an impenetrable barrier protecting her heart. Back off or suffer the consequences!"

It was the first time I had a conversation with Pam that didn't make sense to me. There didn't seem to be a real issue, and there didn't seem to be a way to have a rational discussion. I couldn't defend her siblings or I would make her more upset. I didn't think I could support Pam because I didn't think she was right. Looking back, I realize she needed to know that she was more important to me than anyone else in the room. It was a purely emotional need to know that I valued her. I know that now, but I didn't know it then. I did my best to reassure her, but I ended the trip thinking we hadn't resolved anything.

Since it had to do with her brother and sister, I assumed it wouldn't come home with us. Silly me! We were sitting in our living room one night, and I said something to Pam that apparently hurt her feelings. She jumped up from the couch, shouted, "You don't love me anymore," and ran to our room. I watched in stunned silence as she slammed the door behind her. I waited in the living room to see if she would gather herself together and come back out to talk. After a few minutes, it became apparent that Pam was not coming out, so I decided to venture in. I found her facedown on our bed, sobbing.

Wow, my dad never told me about this!

I wasn't sure what I had done, but it appeared to be a major violation of the "love your wife" principle. I did my best to reassure Pam. I told her, "I love you," numerous times, hoping it would break through her resistance. I assumed I must have done something wrong, so I did my best to find out what it was. Whatever it was never surfaced, but the atmosphere did eventually soften.

I didn't know at the time that the issue was *security*. Pam needed to know that she was safe with me, that I would love her when she made sense and when she didn't. She needed to know that I would engage her in intellectual discussions and that I would love her through irrational interactions.

If I knew then what I know now, I would have simply told Pam over and over that she is safe with me. I would have looked her in the eyes and told her she was secure with me until she believed me.

You Don't Outgrow It

I would love to tell you that Pam has outgrown her security need, but I would be misleading you. The need has become less intense as Pam has matured, but it still comes up for air periodically. For instance, we recently had this conversation about a writing project I'm pursuing.

"Pam, I'm going to be meeting with Tom to lay out a plan to launch the 'Pay Attention' project."

"Why are you doing that with Tom?" Pam asked.

Tom has been a trusted friend of ours for years, so the bite in Pam's voice caught me off guard.

"He gets the idea and has been consistently enthusiastic about the project for a long time. Besides that, he's a very good marketer," I said.

All I got from Pam was silence. The verbal conversation was over, but the body language continued to send messages of dissatisfaction. It took until the next day, but we finally got to the real conversation.

"Bill, you know the awkward conversation we had the other day? Would you like to know what that was about?"

"I sure would! Thanks for offering." (Meaning, "Please, please because I know I will keep paying for it if I can't figure it out and we are on a cruise and I would like sex again while on vacation!")

"When you said you were going to work with Tom, I got my feelings hurt. I thought it meant you didn't want to work with me. I just got kind of jealous. I know it was just my insecurity and I don't need to be threatened. I trust you and I really appreciate Tom. Actually I'm excited to see what happens with this project."

We met the need effectively, but the need still exists. Knowing the code gives us shortcuts into each other's hearts. Small differences don't escalate to all-out wars. Problems are solved faster and with greater intimacy, and we have very few issues arise because overall we make a concerted effort to meet the security and success needs in each other.

I (Pam) also remember when I first became aware that Bill looks at life and love through the lens of success. We had been married about a year, and Bill was acting different when he came home from work. He was quiet and would get frustrated over little things like spills in the kitchen or bills that needed to be paid. I thought it would pass, but it hung on longer than I thought was good, so I asked him, "Bill, what is up? You don't seem to be yourself."

"I don't think I can keep doing this," he said all too quickly.

My fears jumped to the surface. "What do you mean you can't keep doing this? What is 'this'?" ("This" could be anything: this schedule, this apartment, this job, this marriage!)

"I don't think I can keep working at this job. In my heart, I want nothing more than to be in full-time ministry. I need to find a way, but I'm nervous about asking you because it will mean a big sacrifice."

"This is simply about your job? If you want to pursue another career, that's okay with me," I said with relief in my voice.

"Are you sure? It will mean going back to college and eating a lot of hot dogs and beans."

I told Bill that night that I was more than willing to make whatever sacrifices were necessary to help him reach his goals. I had no idea at the time how big an impact my support would have on Bill. His energy level immediately increased. Within a few weeks, he put together a plan to save money for six months, begin a freelance drafting service to pay the bills, and enroll in college to finish his last two years. He was working harder than ever, but he was more encouraging to me than I had previously seen him. He seemed to think I was better looking, more spiritual, and more trustworthy. I knew something important was happening even though at the time I couldn't pinpoint it as an intense need in Bill to succeed.

I thought it was probably just a work thing until the need began to surface in other areas. I noticed that Bill would spend hours working on a project because he had to get it done and get it done right. One year he even made a jewelry box for me with small drawers and glass doors. He spent five days in my grandfather's shop to get it done. I appreciated the gesture of love but was amazed that he could spend that much time on one project while we were on vacation.

Then I began to notice that Bill was pretty sensitive about criticism from me. Other people could point out areas that needed to change, and he would accept it graciously. If I volunteered the same evaluation, he would either get upset or clam up for a few hours. It all seemed silly to me at first, but I have come to realize that Bill is wired to succeed in relationships and pursuits, and when he is succeeding, he is a lot easier to live with.

Just as I have not outgrown my need to be secure, Bill has not outgrown his need to succeed.

Bill has just been through a major transition. After serving in the local church for twenty years, he recently took on the challenge of speaking at churches and conferences and writing full-time. While he served at the church, he enjoyed long-term relationships where he would observe the progress in people's lives week after week. Now, he sees quick change in people's lives over the course of a week or weekend, and then moves to the next location.

I know he is enjoying it, but I also see him struggling with how to succeed at this new ministry. His instincts for the local church worked well; his instincts for freelance work are not as developed. His learning curve is very high, and his discomfort with the process of itinerant ministry is obvious to me. He is handling it better than he would have early in our marriage, but his anxiety is very close to the surface each and every day. He is extremely talented at being a "pastor to pastors" and a "marriage and relationship expert." But the business side of this new full-time lifestyle has some new objectives and goals, and these can sometimes be perceived by Bill as obstacles to success.

I know it is a big struggle for him because he gets offended easily and has to apologize more than he normally does. He spends long hours in his office trying to get caught up with the process of life on the road. He asks me a lot of questions about how to live this kind of life where airports and hotel rooms make up so much of our schedule, and he gets upset if I give him answers that are too short. He also gets upset if I give him answers that are too long. He told me it makes him feel stupid and embarrassed to even have to ask.

It is confusing trying to figure him out right now because this need is so vibrant. I know from experience that he will come to a point where he knows how to make this new life work, and he will transform back into the man I know and love. Just knowing that a man who is on a success learning curve is more sensitive or more focused gives me more patience and grace in relating to Bill at this transitional stage of our love. For me, this knowledge is like having the code to Bill's heart. For now, we will take the journey together, and I will try not to be too critical or take things too personally.

Very few couples have the natural ability to say to one another, "I think we have failed to apply the usernames and passwords that make up the marriage code," but almost all couples can tell when they are out of sync. They find themselves making statements such as:

- "I am confused."
- "This makes me nervous."

- "I am anxious about this."
- "I don't understand."
- "I am frustrated."
- "I just don't know what to do to please you."
- "I feel all alone."
- "I don't know how to approach you."
- "You make me so angry."
- "What's going on here?"
- "I don't really like you much right now."
- "This is driving me crazy!"

These messages are not the problem; they simply point to the problem. Many couples get distracted by these statements. They try to lower their anger or adjust their expectations in vain. Modifying behavior helps most other relationships, but marriage works on a different plane. Marriage is the only relationship that includes intimacy in all areas of life. Your spouse is the only person on earth with whom you will share your heart, your money, your body, your calendar, your decisions, and your fears. The key to getting back on track is to institute the code.

Get Above the Line!

The exclusive nature of marriage creates a fascinating dynamic. The key needs of success and security can be triggered quickly. A wife can instantly feel secure or she can feel instantly insecure. A husband, likewise, can feel suddenly successful or suddenly like a failure.

It's as if you operate in your marriage around a line. When your key need gets met, you move above the line and *everything* seems to work well. You are comfortable in the relationship, you forgive readily, you find it easy to give your spouse the benefit of the doubt, and romance is satisfying.

When your key need gets threatened, you move below the line and *everything* seems to be a problem. The relationship feels awkward and most discussions turn into arguments. You entertain thoughts about your spouse's motives that are petty and selfish while you fight the urge to blame your spouse for your dissatisfaction.

The strangest part of this dynamic is that you can move above the line or below the line very quickly. One word, one action, one look can ruin the atmosphere of your relationship and send you plummeting below the line. Trust is temporarily lost and feelings are bruised. In the same way, one word or action can elevate you above the line, reestablish trust, and normalize the atmosphere in your home.

The moments when you cross above the line create breakthroughs in your relationship that build memories and raise your confidence. And a track record of being above the line creates a buffer or safety zone of grace. Mistakes are not taken so personally. Your spouse reads a mistake as, "Well, she or he meant well," and gives you the benefit of the doubt.

A track record of using the correct password keeps the keycard to your spouse's heart working for a while, usually long enough to adjust and seek to meet the security and success needs in one another. The goal is to get above the line and stay above the line and to build a track record with your spouse of loving over the line.

Our experience is that most couples are one step away from a breakthrough that will make their marriage a very enjoyable partnership. Every time the marriage code is activated in your love, a breakthrough happens. You cannot force the breakthrough to happen because it involves a change of heart in both you and your spouse. You can, however, set up all the elements that make it likely that a breakthrough will take place. The rest of this book explores the practical steps you can take to keep your username and password up-to-date so that you gain access to the best in your relationship.

UNLOCKING THE CODE:
Dinner and Dialogue for a Heart-to-Heart Connection

In each chapter, we will give you a "couple communication exercise" perfect for a heart-to-heart talk over coffee, a meal, or dessert. You might also decide a walk and talk or some in-the-car conversation helps you connect. Wherever you decide to dialogue, these questions and activities are aimed at helping you gain a deeper appreciation of your mate so that security and success can flourish in your home.

In a relaxed environment, share your answers to these questions (no problem solving yet—tonight is for compliments only!)

Wife ask your husband: What things do I do that help you feel more successful?

Husband ask your wife: What things do I do that help you feel more secure?

Wife to husband: What days so far in our relationship have you felt most successful?

Husband to wife: What days so far in our relationship have you felt most secure?

Wife to husband: Thank your husband for the qualities and traits in his life that you most appreciate that build into your sense of security.

Husband to wife: Thank your wife for the qualities and traits in her life that you most appreciate that build into your sense of success.

■ ■ ■

Wives get points for even attempting to keep the bedroom interesting. One of my friends gained bonus points for her attempt at romantic creativity. She sent me this description of her version of the famous Mideastern "Dance of the Seven Veils":

> My husband's birthday was coming up, so I booked a nice hotel for the night to celebrate. I'd been reading in a marriage book that you have to be creative in your sexual life

with your spouse, so I daydreamed of things I could do to spice things up. That's when I got the idea for the dance of the seven veils! On the big night, I went to the bathroom and layered myself in four silk scarves, two swimsuit cover ups, and one winter scarf. I didn't look like a seductress; I looked like a mixed up bag lady! But I charged into that hotel room and pretended to be a belly dancer. My husband didn't lust, he laughed, and we made a fun memory.

ABOVE THE LINE

BELOW THE LINE

Our actions and words can get us in the doghouse pretty quickly, as this couple discovered:

A man and woman were driving home from a social event when a police car pulled up behind them and turned on its lights.

As he pulled the car to the side of the road, the husband, who had a history of controlling behavior, sternly said to his wife, "Follow my lead. Do exactly what I tell you to do."

The policeman walked up to the driver's side window and asked for the man's license and registration. After reviewing the documents, he said, "Sir, are you aware that you've been speeding for a while?"

"No, I wasn't aware of that," the man said. "My speedometer said I was traveling the speed limit. Just ask my wife; she can corroborate."

The policeman looked over at the woman and asked, "Is that true?"

Without hesitation, she said, "Officer, I never argue with my husband when he's been drinking."

Chapter 2

The Mystery of Love

"The fruit of the Spirit is love..."

Good morning, Mr. Phelps..." Those words have inspired TV and movie watchers for three generations. In 1966 the Impossible Mission Force (IMF) took to the airwaves on *Mission: Impossible* to combat dictators and evil organizations. The team was resurrected in 1988 for a second run on television and then again in movie form in the late 1990s. Each movie and each TV episode begins with an unknown boss sending a message about a secret mission on a self-destructing tape to Jim Phelps. The mission was vital. The assignment was filled with danger and intrigue. The task seemed impossible, but somehow the IMF team could always figure out a way to get it done. Imagine your own Mission Impossible assignment when it comes to relationships:

"Good morning, Mr. and Mrs. Modern. *Your mission, should you choose to accept it, is to uncover the mystery of love.* You got married because you were looking for love, companionship, and a partner in the journey of life. You have realized by now that you married someone very different from you. Each of you are made up of a complex mixture of wisdom and short-comings, talent and inconsistencies. Your ability to admire and appreciate each other is one of your main tools for building a successful and secure relationship. Your goal is to remain curious about each other so you can live above the line. We wish you the best on your journey together."

The goal of the marriage code is to get your relationship above the line where you can experience a secure and successful relationship. We've identified eight different skills you can use to build both security and success in your life together. To make these skills easier to remember, we've arranged them as an acrostic for the word *marriage*. You will find security and success in your marriage when you make these eight approaches to life part of your journey:

Mystery of love

Affection

Recreation

Resolving conflicts

Intimacy

Activating the alarms

Golden goals

Expressing yourself

We will explore these skills one by one in the chapters that follow, beginning in this chapter with the mystery of love.

THE MYSTERY OF LOVE

There is a mystery to love that intrigues all of us. You are fascinated with each other and live with the hope that you can discover a relationship that works. Sometimes it is so easy to be with the one you love. You laugh together, plan together, dream together, and love together. At other times, you scratch your head and search for ways to figure each other out. At times you marvel because you are so in sync. You marvel with equal amazement at how intense your conflicts can be.

The mystery exists because you have married someone who is thoroughly different from you. You may have thought at first that you were very similar, but you have since discovered that you look at life from different perspectives.

The Great Things About Men

As a wife, there are things you need to know about your husband if you want him to feel that he can succeed with you. These are traits that probably attracted you to him and drive you crazy at the same time. They are at the core of what it means to be a man, so you will never fully understand them. You can only accept that these are true.

(In our best-selling book, *Men Are Like Waffles, Women Are Like Spaghetti,* we look at many ways men and women are different and how to use those differences to work for you in your marriage. Since the release of that book, we have added to our information on the differences between men and women and some of that information is added here.)

Men are highly emotional but simple when it comes to expressing their emotions. Modern research has revealed that men are just as emotional as women and even feel the stress of the family at a deeper level than their wives. We don't tend to think this because women are more expressive with their emotions. When a woman is upset about something, her mom knows she is upset. Her friends know she is upset. The clerk at the store knows she is upset! Men, on the other hand, have a greater tendency to become flooded with their emotions (overwhelmed by their magnitude and intensity), so they seek to escape rather than face the challenge head on.[2]

Men look for simple solutions. Men have been created with a high level of ability to separate the issues of life and focus on one issue at a time. The male brain is physically designed for this ability. In the womb, high levels of testosterone cause many of the connections between the two sides of the brain to be severed. As a result, when a man focuses on a problem, he uses only one side of his brain. He may use the left side or he may use the right side, but he uses only one side. Men find it easy to settle on a solution and stick with the decision. At the same time, men find it difficult to keep talking about issues and get frustrated when decisions are left open-ended.

Life is more risky for males than for females. It starts in the womb where more male than female children miscarry. It progresses through childhood as more males than females die in infancy. It continues throughout life as men are prone to more diseases since they do not have an extra X chromosome to make up for deficiencies that may exist in the one they do have.[3] Add the aggressive nature of testosterone to this formula, and men naturally take more risks.

Men can shut down their emotions to handle a crisis at hand. A man's ability to compartmentalize his thinking gives him the capacity to minimize the emotional component of a crisis and focus on a pragmatic way to get through it. He can reason his way through the situation without being overtaken by the intense emotions involved.

Men are highly motivated when they believe they can succeed. A man will work long hours, go to great lengths, and invest large amounts of time and money into the pursuits that he reasonably believes he can succeed at. Men make solid commitments to their careers in order to provide for their loved ones. A husband will spend lots of time loving and romancing his wife when he concludes his advances will succeed with her. A father will go out of his way to encourage his kids and give them opportunities for growth when he believes his efforts will be respected and responded to. This is so much a part of who a man is that he has a hard time holding on to his motivation in any area of life in which he concludes he cannot succeed.

The Great Things About Women

Women are good conversationalists. The part of a woman's brain that controls speech is larger than a man's. From her earliest days, she finds conversation to be a very effective tool. She makes friends by talking. She connects with her parents through talking. She gets her way through conversations. She relieves stress with words. She is physically wired to fill her life with words and feels valued when her words are treated as important.

Women can multitask better than men. The multitude of connections between the two sides of a female brain gives her the ability to unite the various issues of life in a seamless flow. She can tie together intellectual, emotional, spiritual, and social issues with very little effort.

She doesn't even have to "try" to connect them; it comes to her naturally.

Women are less surprised by change than men. Life is more complex for females as their hormones are in constant flux. It begins with menstruation and its miserable cousin, PMS. In doing research for my book, *Fantastic After 40!*, I (Pam) discovered these hormones transition into menopause with a possibility of nearly 100 symptoms in a woman's most productive years. Just when you get PMS down it morphs into menopause!

Women are more active than men in bringing up issues in marriage. This doesn't mean that women are better at bringing up issues, just that they react sooner. Many times a woman doesn't even know what the issue is; she simply can sense there is one. Her instincts tell her that something is not right. Her intuition screams inside her that something needs to change. In response, she makes noise. Many husbands mistakenly think she must know what the problem is because she is speaking with such force when, in reality, she may have no better insight into the issue than her husband does. This is why many issues go unresolved for the average couple. She brings up the issue. He reacts to the content of her concern, which is not really the issue. They argue without identifying the issues at hand so no real resolution surfaces.

Women have a higher sense of urgency about the needs of the family. From an early date, moms dream about their kids' futures, their spouses, and the children they will have some day. They sense how the actions of today will affect their kids' development tomorrow. As a result, even the smallest things can feel like a big deal because of the far-reaching potential. For this reason, women often have urgent reactions to situations that take their loved ones by surprise.

I (Bill) was recently in a business meeting with a group of women who were planning an event. I was overseeing the budget for the event, and the husband of one of the ladies in the meeting was providing audiovisual for the event. I mentioned that I had not received the A/V bid yet so I could not finish the budget. I then said that I would call him after the meeting and e-mail the budget to everyone as soon as

I had it done. In a meeting of men, they would have said, "OK, get back to us as soon as you have it finished."

But I wasn't in a meeting of men. The man's wife immediately pulled out her cell phone and called her husband. "Bill needs to get the budget finished. He needs our bid right now. No, he can't wait. He is only waiting on you."

I tried to tell everyone there was no rush, and I would make the call after the meeting. My efforts, however, were to no avail. The urgency got so frantic that I had to dismiss myself from the meeting, call the A/V provider, and get the budget completed. It was a good reminder that God made women very different from me![4]

> **Decoder Moment:** Take a moment to stop here and chat about the gender differences that you appreciate most in your mate.

It Is Amazing!

These differences are based on the levels of estrogen and testosterone in your body. Of course, you have learned to adapt to life as you have matured so you are not at the whim of your hormones, but your hormones will never change. You have all the benefits and liabilities of your gender. As a result, you will always be fascinated with each other and you will never fully understand each other. You are so different from each other that you will always be mystified by the way your mate makes decisions, the way he or she responds to things, and the preferences that captivate your spouse's heart.

These differences give your relationship great potential because your spouse brings to your life what you don't have on your own. At the same time, these differences produce significant stress because you must adjust to an approach to life that you would never bring to your own life.

You married each other because you are fascinated with each other. For this reason, your spouse has more influence over you than anyone you have ever met. In fact, your partner can affect you in ways that no one else in your world can even get close to.

Consider how many of these ways you have responded to your wife:

- She smiles at you, and you instantly soften.
- She flirts with you, and you feel suddenly younger.
- She puts her hands on your shoulders to gently rub your back, and every muscle in your body tingles.

Or

- She gives you "the look," and your blood runs cold.
- She tells you how to address a problem in your home, and you feel instantly insulted.
- She comments on a decision you made, and you grow intensely angry.
- She makes fun of you in public, and you quickly conclude she has no respect for you.
- She nags you for things she wants, and you erupt in criticism and name calling.

Consider how many of these ways you have responded to your husband:

- He gives you a hug, and you melt into his arms.
- He gives you a romantic gift, and all of life is suddenly bright and sunny.
- He calls you during the day for no reason, and everything seems easier for the rest of the day.

Or

- He forgets to do an errand you asked him to do, and you feel personally offended and devalued.
- He criticizes you for something minor around the house, and your day is shattered.

- He raises his voice to you, and your defenses spring to action.
- He says you are controlling, and your anger hits the roof.
- He laughs at you, and you erupt in anger as you think he devalues everything about you.

The Choice

The intense influence you have on each other creates a vulnerable atmosphere in your home. It changes from happy to hectic to irritating back to happy in moments. One look, one comment, one action can alter the environment of your relationship for either good or bad. A number of steps will help you harness the dynamic influence you have on each other and get it to work for you.

Step 1: Accept your differences. When you make it your goal to understand each other, you will most likely find yourself frustrated and confused. Men will never understand women because they will never experience the constant change and persistent urgency that dominates a woman's life. Women, likewise, will never understand the aggressive, risky journey that men take every day. On the other hand, when couples seek to accept each other, they gain fresh insight into each other's lives every week they spend together. They never fully reach the point of understanding, but they experience a deeper, richer relationship over time.

Step 2: Deal with you. Your reactions to your spouse create at least half of the environment in your relationship. We say "at least half" because every intimate relationship is a combination of actions and reactions. When you are negative, your spouse has to decide how to respond.

> You are the only one who can be you on earth!

If he or she responds negatively, the tension multiplies. If he or she responds positively, peace may maintain itself for a while. In most cases, a negative response produces a negative response, so the irritation in the home tends to escalate. You can minimize the negative by keeping yourself moving in a healthy direction.

The Influence of You

Consider the influence of your life:

- You are the only one who can determine your attitude.
- You are the only one who knows the thoughts that go on in your head.
- You are the only one who fully experiences the range of emotions that go on in your heart.
- You are the only one who can be the husband to your wife or wife to your husband.
- You are the only one who can be the father or mother of your children.
- You are the only one who can be you on earth!

The problem is that you are complicated.

- You are hardest on the one you love the most.
- You guard your heart from the one you want to be closest to.
- You criticize the one who once captivated your imagination.
- You pull away when you ought to be pulling together.
- You are afraid and courageous all at the same time.

Too often, instead of building into each other's natural gender inclinations and preferences, we complain and fight against God's creative agenda. Like these students, we can get a downright negative attitude about the opposite gender:

> An English professor wrote the words: "Woman without her man is nothing" on the blackboard and directed the students to punctuate it correctly. The men wrote: "Woman, without her man, is nothing." The women wrote: "Woman! Without her, man is nothing."

Are you sensing a negative attitude developing? A college student named Steve writes,

> As a senior at St. Cloud State University in Minnesota, I often engage women psychology majors in heated discussions about male-female relationships. Once, my friend Shelly and I got into a hot debate about whether men or women make the larger sacrifice of their respective gender characteristics when they get married. To my surprise, Shelly agreed with me that men give up far more than women.
>
> "You're right, Steve," she said. "Men generally give up doing their cleaning, their cooking, their grocery shopping, and their laundry."

Step 3: Raise each other's energy level: Gaining insight into how genders work will enable you to operate more freely and motivate each other more readily. A man's energy level will rise when he is confident he can succeed, feels he has been heroic, is reasonably certain sexual activity will be part of the near future, and his life is relatively simple. Conversely, his energy level will fall when he concludes he cannot succeed no matter how hard he tries, sexual activity is threatened, and life gets more complicated than his capacity to process.

> A man's energy level will rise when he is confident he can succeed.

Raise His Energy Level

As a result, a wife can help raise her husband's energy level if she:

- Sincerely and regularly compliments her husband.
- Flirts with her husband.
- Puts sexual activity on her calendar so she is deliberately in the mood.
- Helps her husband know when the conversation is just a journey and when they are working toward a decision or the solution to a problem.

- Does anything that makes his life simpler. This is a challenge because women's lives are inherently more complex than a man's. Her menstrual cycle guarantees that her life is constantly changing physically, and the interconnectedness of her life ensures that her life is constantly changing emotionally. Nevertheless, when she sticks to commitments and relieves any stress from her husband's life, his energy level rises.

Raise Her Energy Level

A woman's energy level rises when she feels she is valued for who she is and what she contributes to the lives of those who are important to her. She is highly productive if she feels she is functioning in a safe environment. She is remarkable at seeing the connections in life, and it all gets a little overwhelming on a regular basis. She is aware of her husband's mannerisms, moods, and mistakes. She senses how this will affect her friendships, her confidence, and her schedule. If she has kids, she is aware of their schedules, their needs, their preferences, their academic progress, and their ability to interact successfully in social settings. In her heart, she carries responsibility for making sure that everyone in her family loves God, discovers their strengths, and has friends.

> A woman's energy level rises when she feels she is valued for who she is.

Simply stated, she carries the weight of her world on her shoulders. She would prefer not to, but she can't seem to escape the perception that life is one connected story and every scene requires her attention. As a result, she can feel pretty insignificant as she fights to keep up with the mounting expectations and challenges of life. She longs to know that she is important and that her life is making a difference to those she cares about.

A husband can raise his wife's energy level by:

- Listening to her with fascination
- Noticing her as she walks by, when she changes her clothes, when she gets her hair done, when she wakes up

- Thanking her for the things she has done today
- Complimenting her for anything—the way she looks, the way she works, the way she takes care of you and the family
- Listening to her with fascination
- Discovering her love language and paying special attention to speaking that language[5]
- Planning romantic encounters for her
- Spending time with her—walk and talk, share a cup of coffee, do errands together without complaining
- Providing the basic necessities (food, shelter, love, friendship) so she feels secure and safe

Vive la Différence

We spend a lot of time and energy complaining about the differences even though we cannot change them. To be sure, we all need to grow and mature so we are a better version of ourselves with each passing year, but there is no way to change the basics of being male and female.

For instance, one study reveals that when a man eats, the part of his brain that makes him feel happier is stimulated. When a woman eats, the part of her brain that sharpens her eyesight is stimulated. She is more aware of her environment and has more to talk about. This is why so many good relationship moments happen around food.[6] Grandma was right! A way to a man's heart *is* through his stomach. (This is also a helpful study to know about if you wreck your husband's car. Just feed him his favorite meal first, then tell him about the car.)

If we tap into the way God hardwired us and accept these differences in gender, we can help raise the energy level in our relationships. If we fight against nature, our mate might feel we are fighting against them, and that is an energy drain. Revel and rejoice in the gender differences to keep motivation and energy high in your marriage.

The Heart of the Matter

Step 4: Develop a relationship of grace. Remember, the goal is to create a relationship where you can feel secure and successful so you can live above the line of turmoil. The problem is that we are all imperfect. As men, we will never get everything right, so our sense of success is easily challenged. As women, we regularly fall short of our intentions, so our sense of being secure with those we love most is hard to hold on to.

> If we tap into the way God hardwired us and accept these differences in gender, we can help raise the energy level in our relationships.

You need a way to direct the best of who you are so that it builds into your marriage, and you need a way to contain the parts of you that tend to get in the way of your relationships.

Aspects of an Intimate Relationship

The atmosphere that characterizes a successful marriage is described in Philippians 1:7, where Paul tells the church at Philippi: "It is right for me to feel this way about all of you, since I have you in my heart; for whether I am in chains or defending and confirming the gospel, all of you share in God's grace with me." Three important aspects of an intimate relationship come to light from this passage.

The GOAL

The goal of intimacy is to hold each other in your hearts. There is a special connection that is possible between two people. When this connection is achieved, all of life works better. There is harmony, anticipation, and a sense that it is easy to be around each other. You give each other the benefit of the doubt because you already have each other in your heart. When this connection is interrupted, spouses begin to judge each other based on behavior. "You didn't do this. You did that," becomes the most frequently quoted statement in the couple's conversations. Since everyone's behavior is inconsistent, the relationship suffers greatly when it is based on behavior. That is why relationships lose their satisfaction when life becomes a series of shared tasks rather than a pursuit of each other's hearts.

Pam and I have experienced both sides of this journey numerous times. The first time we became aware of the power of the words, "I have you in my heart," happened during the second year of our marriage. I (Bill) had decided to return to college to finish my undergraduate degree. Shortly after making that decision, our car failed. I was working from our home, so I could "get to work" without driving. I was willing to ride my bike to school, but I felt bad asking Pam to ride her bike to work. It felt very unfair for me to even ask her, and it wouldn't have taken much to make me feel like I was failing as a husband.

In a courageous step, Pam said to me, "I trust you, Bill, because you are in my heart. We will work this out."

It was awesome to hear those words. My motivation to finish school with good grades so I could be a good provider intensified and gave me renewed energy. Pam could easily have criticized me for the financial shortcomings, but she chose instead to keep me in her heart. As a result, I was able to finish my bachelor's degree and my master's degree and assist Pam in obtaining her college degree.

The GLUE

The glue for this connection is a partnership of grace. Paul was intensely aware of his shortcomings. Prior to his dramatic conversion on the road to Damascus, Paul was intent on arresting the followers of Christ and doing all he could to shut down the church. Then he met the true love of his life. He fell in love with the one he had been seeking to destroy. As a result, he lived with a profound realization that he had been forgiven immensely and given the gift he least deserved.

Relationships thrive best under grace. You are guaranteed to make mistakes. Your spouse is guaranteed to make mistakes. It doesn't take long until you realize that you can't behave good enough for long enough to earn the love of your spouse. You have probably done some great things for your partner, but at the same time you have said and done things that should not be part of a loving relationship. These mistakes have the potential to destroy the emotional connection between you. At the same time, each of your shortcomings creates an opportunity to establish grace. The result of grace is a belief that this relationship is safe.

It is challenging when you slip out of each other's hearts. We saw this clearly one night when I (Bill) was leading a baptism service at the beach—this meant we were the "spiritual leaders" of the group that night. Pam had a speaking engagement the next day, so she was planning on heading home early.

We had finished the baptism and shared a barbecued meal together. Our three boys grabbed their boogey boards and asked if they could head out into the water. I said yes and walked into the water about knee deep to keep a watch on them. Pam joined me in the water, and we were sharing a good conversation when she suddenly said, "Bill, we need to get the boys out of the water because I need to leave."

I was confused because only Pam was leaving. I had handled the boys on my own time and again. Did Pam not trust me? Had I done something wrong that I was not aware of? I plunged "under the line" in our relationship in an instant.

"You can go ahead, Pam," I said.

"I know, but we have to get the boys out of the water first."

"Why do we have to get the boys out?"

"Because I'm leaving."

"Yeah, but I'm not."

"Well, I am and I know how you get. You are going to get distracted. People are going to want to talk to you, and the boys will probably float away to Hawaii."

"How did Hawaii get into this discussion?" I blurted out with a rise in my voice.

"I just know how distracted you get, and I'm trying to protect the kids."

I turned to Pam and said, "Let me see if I understand this correctly. You've trusted me to take our boys to Mexico without you, but you don't think I can watch over them at the beach that is closest to our home. Is that what you're saying to me?"

It was a weird moment for us. Pam didn't feel like she could trust me, and I couldn't believe that I had fallen out of grace with her so quickly. It felt to me like I was back with my mom who was afraid of almost everything and refused to trust anyone. Pam had judged me inadequate, and I had concluded she didn't make sense. This was strange for us because we were used to giving each other the benefit of the doubt. This night, however, we were giving nothing but doubt.

Pam looked me in the eyes as her facial features softened. "Oh my, I probably sound like your mom right now, don't I?"

"You said it, Pam, not me."

"I am sorry, Bill. Our baggage just collided. I struggled to trust my alcoholic father growing up, and I have put that on you. You struggled to trust your fearful mom, and I can tell that got triggered in you. I am going to head home and just trust you with the kids. I will see you later."

We were able to do this because we had worked through forgiving our parents, and we had committed to aggressively forgiving each other whenever it was necessary.[7] Just as quickly as we had fallen out of each other's hearts, we drifted right back in. The difference was staggering. Under the line, there was a lack of trust and strange thoughts about what the other might do. We quickly started evaluating each other's motives and reached unhealthy conclusions about each other. Above the line, everything settled down. The attraction to each other reappeared, and the encounter began to be humorous almost instantly.

The GROWTH

Once a partnership of grace is formed, a partnership of purpose can be established. Paul's purpose was "the defense and proclamation of the gospel." The church in Philippi had a special interest in this pursuit because of their personal connection with Paul. The same can be true in your marriage. When you establish a connection of grace, you unleash the power of your lives. You are free to think, feel, and dream. You are internally motivated to encourage each other because you value the relationship so much. Ideas can flow freely because criticism is rare. You can take risks because trust is high. These are all the elements of success, and they naturally result in marriages that have discovered grace and purpose.

We began to discover our purpose together during the first four years of our marriage. You have heard that we grew up in tough homes, so when we married each other, we knew two things: (1) We loved each other, and (2) we didn't really know what we were doing. In desperation, we sought out what we believed was solid advice.

We would go to church each weekend and stand at the back of the church until the service began. As we were in the back, we would scan the audience looking for couples who had been married for a while and still liked each other. We assumed that a couple who was holding hands, leaning on each other, or sitting with one of their arms around the shoulder of the other was a good candidate. We would sit right behind these couples so they had to meet us during the greeting time of the service.

> When you establish a connection of grace, you unleash the power of your lives.

I (Bill) would ask them, "You look like you really love each other. Is that for real?"

Every one of these couples responded the same. They would laugh a little, look at each other and say, "Yes. Our love is for real."

I would then ask, "How did you do it? How did you manage to stay in love after being together all these years?"

The couple didn't have time to answer the question during the greeting time, so they would almost always ask us out to lunch. At lunch, we would ask them questions and listen to them recount the story of their lives together. Some of the best advice we have ever received came from these informal meals with real couples sharing their real experiences. For instance:

- Take sarcasm out of your marriage.
- Laugh together every day.
- Make your spouse your best friend.

- Never stop treating your wife like your girlfriend.
- Never stop flirting with your husband.
- Call your spouse from work just to say, "I love you."
- Couples who pray together stay together.
- Keep dating.
- The best gift you can give your kids is a happy, secure marriage.

We never thought these curiosity lunches would turn into a ministry to couples and parents. We just knew that we needed to know how to be successfully married. We have often told these couples, "The impact we have had on marriages developed because you took a young couple out to lunch."

Decoder Moment: Each of you share your answer to this: So far, what advice has someone older and wiser given you on marriage that you have seen rings true?

The Mystery of Growth

In establishing an atmosphere of grace, it is important to note that growth in our lives is a tricky thing. Some areas change quickly. These areas are exciting to talk about and fulfilling to work on because the results are tangible and quick. Other areas of our lives are slow-growth traits. Change in these areas happens slowly no matter how much focus and effort we put into them. These areas especially need grace in order to create a safe atmosphere in your relationship.

What areas of your life are slow-growth areas for which you hope your spouse will give you grace?

Example: I (Bill) have always struggled with getting home on time. I tend to get caught up with people and lose track of time. I have worked on writing out my schedule, reviewing my schedule the night before, and setting reminders on my computer and cell phone. None of them has made the struggle disappear. Thankfully, Pam has been very patient with me as I have sought to improve.

Example: I (Pam) am a woman on a mission, so I love the front side of life—dreaming, planning, preparing—but I'm not so excited about the backside of life—filing, balancing the checkbook, receipts, and invoicing. Bill has given me much grace in this area and has made some practical steps to take the irritation out of our relationship in this slow-growth area. One simple example is that I used to forget to record a check in the register, so he solved that by ordering duplicate checks that create a copy automatically as you write the check. He doesn't have to nag me or get upset if I forget, and I don't have to remember anymore!

What areas of your spouse's life are slow-growth areas and need your grace in order to create a safe environment in your relationship?

Example: Pam is passionate about her career and has a hard time "looking behind her." She tends to leave lights on, forgets to finish the laundry, periodically runs out of gas, and misplaces her possessions. She is an exciting woman to live with as long as I consider this a minor trait.

Example: Bill is a highly productive male who loves his coffee. I find coffee cups everywhere: the garage, the car, the office. One day I noticed our cabinet was getting low on coffee mugs, so I grabbed a box and went through every room in our home, the garage, all cars, and his office. I gathered up 17 mugs that Bill meant to bring into the kitchen, but they hadn't arrived yet. Rather than get irritated, I chose to see this as a humorous quirk of his that produces his high-octane life.

The Right Kind of Effort

To be sure, marriage takes effort, but your relationship is not all about effort. The amount of effort you put into your marriage is not the key to a great marriage. The amount of effort is not nearly as important as the type of effort you pursue. Consider the following:

- If your car needs oil, it doesn't matter how much effort you put into washing, waxing, and detailing it. The engine still needs oil.

- If the plumbing in your house needs to be unclogged, it doesn't matter how much effort you put into cleaning the windows and mowing the lawn. The plumbing still needs to be unclogged.

- If your hair needs to be restyled, it doesn't matter how much time you spend reorganizing your wardrobe. Your hair still needs to be restyled.

I think you get the point. The more strategic your activity, the more effective the results will be. Conversely, the more distracted your activity, the more frustrating your efforts will be. The purpose of this book is to help you be more strategic in how you work on your marriage. We hope to help you avoid distractions, focus your efforts, and uncover the code that unlocks the potential in your relationship.

UNLOCKING THE CODE:
Dinner and Dialogue for a Heart-to-Heart Connection

Choose a trait based on your spouse's gender and compliment him or her every day for a week. You can deliver the compliments verbally, through e-mail, voicemail, through written notes, or text messages. The key is to do it daily.

Deliberately assign a trait in your spouse's life to the "slow growth" category. Decide that this area of his or her life will change slowly over time, much as the areas in your life that have been agonizingly slow in their development. You are aware of these areas in you because you live with them every day. You have prayed about them, and they don't move at the pace you would like. You have tried to discipline your life in these areas, and you finally concluded that they could grow, but it will probably take the rest of your life.

It's easy to want more from your spouse. Since you have no control over your spouse's growth and development, it's tempting to put pressure on him or her to get better. You can stretch your patience level by choosing to let this area grow at whatever pace it can. If you choose to do this, you cannot complain about it or make unsolicited suggestions about it.

> The amount of effort you invest is not nearly as important as the type of effort you pursue.

Each of you decide what area you are going to give grace and allow God's growth pace. Don't tell your mate which area you have selected; instead, just begin to extend grace in that one area and pray that you will see your mate from God's point of view. As you give this "unnamed gift," look for positive results in your marriage in God's timing instead of your own.

■ ■ ■

One of my friends shared a dinner-party story of a winning sense of humor in her usually quiet, conservative spouse who went outside his comfort zone to bring a smile:

> We had just seen the movie *Far and Away* with Tom Cruise and Nicole Kidman. It had a scene in it where she was his nurse or caregiver, and she had to bathe him. She or her mother or someone else (I can't remember specific details here) put a bowl over his private parts while she washed him (he was unconscious). But then she privately peeked under the bowl with her eyes very wide.
>
> Several weeks later my husband threw a surprise fortieth birthday party for me. He is normally reserved and quiet. When it was time for him to give me my gift, he lay down on the floor with a large mixing bowl you know where (but his clothes were on), and my present was under the bowl. It was hilarious.

Wife: "Honey, there's trouble with the car. It has water in the carburetor."

Husband: "Water in the carburetor? That's ridiculous."

Wife: "Really, Sweetheart, the car has water in the carburetor."

Husband: "You don't even know what a carburetor is. I'll check it out. Where's the car?"

Wife: "In the pool."

Chapter 3

Affection

"The fruit of the Spirit is...kindness..."

O ne of the key elements in a marriage that is secure and successful is affection. We were sharing dinner with a couple at the Walter Reed Hospital in Washington, D.C. The husband was in the wounded soldier brigade because of injuries he suffered in the Iraqi war. He told us how he hiked for miles with his backpack even though he had broken his collarbone, dislocated both shoulders and suffered a back injury and a fractured ankle. We, of course, were amazed at this man's suffering and determination, but what he said next was probably the best moment of his life.

"I may have broken some bones and had some joints out of place, but nothing was going to prevent me from getting back to my wife and children. They are the people I love the most on earth, and my wife is the best thing that has ever happened to me. The enemy tried to break my body, but I determined they would not break my will. I was coming home to my wife and family."

His wife teared up, reached out and held his hand, then turned to us and said, "I have never heard him say this, and I needed to hear those words."

You have been created to respond to affection. It makes you feel stronger, more confident, and attractive. It can calm your heart in a crisis and prepare you for the challenges before you. One of the reasons you married each other is that you discovered someone who made you feel better about yourself. Marriages that are healthy, where you are confident that you can be secure and succeed, are characterized by mutual affection. You go out of your way to compliment one another. You find ways to encourage each other.

You can cultivate affection in your marriage by kindly touching one another, by focusing on your spouse's unique ability, and by showering your relationship with kind words.

KIND PHYSICAL TOUCH

We have all been created to be in physical contact with others. It begins with infants. Babies who are held a lot in an affectionate manner are healthier in all ways. Their immune systems work better, their heart rates and blood pressure are lower, their digestive systems function better, and they are emotionally more balanced.[8]

Things don't change just because we get older. As adults, we still benefit from tender physical touch. Just like kids, adults who have healthy physical interaction with others are physically, emotionally, and socially better balanced. Married couples tend to be in almost constant physical contact with each other early in their relationship. As the relationship matures and responsibilities rise, physical contact tends to fall off. This trend ought to be resisted.

I (Pam) remember when I became aware of the power of physical touch in our marriage. I have always struggled with a fear of failing. My dad was seldom satisfied with anyone's performance, so I learned early in life to overanalyze my actions. Whenever it feels that my plate is too full and something is about to drop, I get pushy, persistent, and turn into a bit of a drama queen. I used to get a Chicken Little, "The sky is falling, the sky is falling!" attitude going. I grew angry with people who wouldn't jump in to rescue me. I perceived their lack of action as disrespect. And did I add that I usually wouldn't voice my fear or my need for help? I just expected those who loved me to magically read my mind and just know I needed them to jump in and bail me out!

One day I was ranting and raving in the kitchen, barking out orders to Bill and the kids, when God pulled back the curtain of my heart and let Bill see straight into my soul. Bill came over and wrapped his arms around me and whispered, "Pam, what are you afraid of?" I struggled to get free so my drama-queen arms could flail and express my pent-up emotion, but Bill wouldn't let me go. "Honey," he whispered again, "what are you afraid of?"

And out streamed a laundry list of fears.

He just kept his arms around me, calming my arms, heart, and soul. It wasn't the kind of holding that was forceful, as if he were demanding something from me. It was an adamant hug that told me we were in this together. Then he kept whispering in my ear, "Pam, I love you. I will always love you. I am your biggest fan. I am here for you. The kids and I, we are here for you. God is here for you. We all want you to succeed. We are on your team. Tell us what we can do to help you feel like the success you are."

I melted into his arms and buried my face in his chest. The weight of the world seemed lifted off my shoulders. I knew a breakthrough had happened, not only emotionally but spiritually too. I didn't have to believe the lie, "You're not good enough." I knew God had proclaimed me "good enough." At eight I had begun a personal relationship with the God of the Universe, who called me his chosen daughter. Intellectually I knew I was good enough for heaven because of God's sacrificial gift of love toward me. But there in my kitchen, after the meltdown of the year, I actually *felt* good enough. It was God's unconditional love sent through Bill that broke the chain of bondage to my past.

My fear of failure could have ruined every relationship I ever had because it makes me so hard on myself. I tend to cast that same stress on others, making demands that are at times unrealistic. Of course, Satan still tries to trip me up with that same old lie, "You're not adequate. You fall short. You're not good enough." But now I fight it better. When I become aware of the fear rising, I take my stand in Christ and declare, "But I am! So leave me and our love alone. Get out. Fear begone!" And fear flees because fear does not function well where love flourishes.

Men, it is important to keep in mind that physical touch is attractive to your wife because it makes her feel secure with you. If you are tender and reassuring when you hold her hand, give her a hug, or snuggle on the couch, she will highly value this part of your relationship. On the other hand, if she concludes you are trying to get something from her or just trying to stay out of trouble with her, she will feel manipulated and conclude it's not safe to be physically intimate with you. It's all about making her feel secure in her relationship with you.

I (Bill) know that we men love to be touched also. We secretly hope you ladies never fully figure out how much power you have in our lives when you love us physically. It all starts with flirting. When a woman touches her husband in a flirtatious way, things change immediately in his heart. He feels stronger, more capable, and more manly. His motivation increases, and his interest in the relationship grows.

I am amazed after three decades of being married how powerful this still is in our relationship. When Pam walks by me and touches me in a tender way, I become instantly distracted in the best possible way. I think, *Wow, she is such a good woman. I am so fortunate to be married to her. I am a stronger man because she is in my life, and she is so cute!*

It happens so quickly that I sometimes think I must be incredibly shallow to respond like this. Her influence in this way is so intense that it even works when I'm upset with her. If things are tense in our relationship and she gives me that flirtatious touch, the words are slightly different but the reaction is the same: *Oh my, she's doing it again. I love it when she touches me like that, but why did she do it now. She must want something from me. Oh, come on, Bill. You're being silly. She's an amazing woman, and she just doesn't know what to do with you right now. She's trying to reach out to you. Let it happen!*

As men, we are often accused of touching our wives only because we want to have sex with them. Most men are more reasonable than this and know that consistent touch in the relationship is more than just having a sexual relationship. As a man, I have to admit the thought that this could lead to a sexual encounter is always present. After all, why not? If she is interested, why wouldn't I be? But I know that the needs in our marriage are more complex than that. Pam needs to be held and know that I am interested in her as a whole person. I need to be hugged and know that Pam is interested in who I am.

The real reason men stop touching their wives is they get criticized when they try. Remember, a man is motivated by success in his marriage. If he feels his attempts to encourage his wife physically are accepted, he is motivated to keep pursuing. If he is criticized each time he reaches out to her, he will eventually stop doing it.

Decoder Moment: Share with each other how you would end these statements:

When you touch me, I feel as if I could…

My favorite way you touch me is…

FOCUS ON UNIQUE ABILITIES

You are an incredibly talented person and you live with incredibly talented people. Each of you has been created with at least one unique ability that gives you remarkable potential. Your unique abilities are strong and demand expression. As a result, they are both incredible and inconvenient. When your unique abilities are focused and you express them with humility, they add a lot to your life. When your unique abilities are undisciplined and expressed with selfishness, they are irritating and can even be damaging.

Your unique abilities are so central to who you are that you have no choice but to build your life around them. When you exercise your unique abilities, you feel more like yourself than at any other time. As a result, you are drawn to people who appreciate your unique contribution to life.

Part of your mission is to identify the unique abilities of your spouse and compliment them as often as possible. These compliments will create a foundation of trust and confidence in your spouse. If you have children, complimenting their unique abilities has the same kind of influence on them. Everyone is more confident. Everyone is more positive. Everyone is more productive.

> You are an incredibly talented person and you live with incredibly talented people.

Men, what your wife wants more than anything else is to feel valued. She wants to know that she is important, and she wants to know that what she does for others is cherished. She is intensely connected to the important people in her life, and she consistently wants to know that her advice, her efforts, and her investment in their lives is making their lives better. When she hears from her loved ones that she is making a difference, she rises above the line of security.

Decoder Moment for Men: Create a way to tell your wife she is a positive difference maker and that your life (or the family, the community, the church, the world) is better for having her in it.

Ladies, what your husband wants to feel more than anything else is that you believe in him. He carries a deep burden for his family, even though he may not express it very well. He wants to love you and provide for his family while he is agonizingly aware of his shortcomings. He knows he should not let his ego get the better of him, but he is easily embarrassed and frustrated when things don't go well. As a result, he longs to have someone in his life who loves him and believes in him. His confidence is greatly enhanced when his wife is attracted to him and compliments him.

Decoder Moment for Women: Create a way to tell your husband you believe in him (his talents, gifts, strength, love, responsibility, character).

Remarkable Talents

Since God is a remarkable creator, you have been "fearfully and wonderfully made" (Psalm 139:14). You are a reflection of His image

(Genesis 1:27). As a result, you possess skills and natural talents. In addition, the Spirit of God provides gifts to everyone who has trusted in Christ as Savior (1 Corinthians 12). The result of all this is that you are proficient in some areas of life while you struggle in other areas.

The idea of unique abilities is easy to conceptualize but challenging to apply. The concept is that you have been created with natural talents that function very well. When you exercise these natural talents, you are proficient and confident. You enjoy operating in your unique abilities and are highly effective when your talents are being applied. The same applies to spiritual gifts. Since they are God-given and empowered by the Holy Spirit, they are effective as they influence others to be stronger and more focused. When your spiritual gift is in action, wisdom flows and the associated tasks seem easy. These thoughts, however, don't tell you how to find your unique abilities or how to apply them in real life.

Finding the Clues to Uniqueness

Your unique ability forms a treasure in you that was designed to make a difference in your world. The problem is that the treasure is hidden. Sometimes we feel we might need our own Indiana Jones, who can interpret clues etched in hieroglyphics. Other times we wish we had a map, as in *National Treasure* where a hidden map was written on the back of the Declaration of Independence. While we might not have a professor of ancient history on retainer, we do have a map coded to lead us to our treasure. The map is written on our hearts by God's Spirit. We just need to tap into His leading to discover the treasure.

> Your unique ability forms a treasure in you that was designed to make a difference in your world.

As a child, you became aware that something in you longed to be expressed. It was powerful, so you looked for ways to live it out; but it was immature, so you were often awkward with it. The world was cruel, so you were criticized and made fun of as you tried to discover who you were and how you were supposed to impact the world. Some of you faced the challenge with thick skin and ignored most of the criticism. You have grown in confidence as you tenaciously pushed through the barriers to your development. Some of you were much more sensitive to the ridicule. You felt crushed as a child, and you are still struggling to find your place. You are afraid to explore new possibilities because the criticism is still fresh in your soul. You would rather just do what you are comfortable with because it is safe, even if it is boring.

The first step to living out your unique abilities is to identify what they are, which is a challenge since there is a significant barrier to discovering what you do best. This *barrier is the unlimited creativity of our creator.* It has been well established that there has never been anyone exactly like you. We all have unique fingerprints, voice prints, and DNA. The same is true of unique abilities. There has never been anyone with the exact collection of wisdom, talents, and intuition that you naturally possess. There is, therefore, no list of unique abilities that you can choose from to identify what you are best at. Instead, you are on a journey that will unfold a piece at a time as you gradually discover both your talents and your purpose. Although there is not a list of unique talents, there are categories in which they operate. Your unique ability is a combination of traits from each of these categories.

Category 1: Physical Aptitudes

You are a physical being made up of bones, muscles, connecting tissue, and nerves. The activities of your body are coordinated by your brain, the most sophisticated computer in the world. The brain constantly sends impulses to the rest of your body instructing it in both voluntary and nonvoluntary movements. As your mind organizes your movements, you discover that you are really good at some things while you are "all thumbs" at others.

Some of you are great with the do-it-yourself trend rampant in our world today. You like to build and repair things. You are even amazed at your ability to figure out unique solutions to physical challenges. Others of you should avoid home repairs at all costs because you make things worse every time you touch a tool. Every attempt to save money by doing it yourself ends up costing a lot more as you hire people to fix your mistakes.

Some of you are naturally talented in small motor skills. You may be a crafter or technician with dexterity in sewing, knitting, quilting, or manufacturing. You may be a professional who uses your gentle touch in surgery or in the production of delicate electronic equipment. You have a steady hand and can navigate intricate movements with skill. Your touch might be used in applying makeup, massage, or the decorative flair. When others attempt to do what you do easily, they destroy the very thing they are trying to fix or create. What you find easy, they find impossible.

> Some of you are great with the do-it-yourself trend rampant in our world today. Others of you should avoid home repairs at all costs.

Others of you are natural at sports and physical activities such as dance or movement. Your confidence on the playing field gives you confidence in life. Being in shape seems the only way to live, and while others avoid things that make them sweat, your life feels empty without such exertion.

You can encourage someone with strong physical aptitudes through the following actions:

- Compliment his ability to fix or build things.
- Thank her for fixing or building something for you.
- Protect his schedule so projects do not get interrupted.
- Spend time admiring the work she has done.
- Allow time for him to enjoy physical activity.
- Join her in an activity even if you feel out of your comfort zone, and ask for her insights.

You will discourage someone with strong physical aptitudes through the following actions:

- Complain about how long the projects take and how much they cost.

- Interrupt the projects every few minutes.

- Tell her how to do things rather than turn the project over to her to figure it out.

- Fill life with paperwork and social commitments so there is little time for projects.

- Over schedule life so little time is left for physical activities.

- Complain that because you don't enjoy physical activity, your spouse or family member shouldn't like it or do it either.

Category 2: Wisdom and Insight

Our minds work incredibly well. They put together thoughts and makes conclusions about life. Some of you, however, have an unusual ability to understand some area of life. You may have insight into business practices that make complex processes simple. You may have wisdom about decision-making that gives you the ability to coach others in their pursuits. You may have understanding about financial operations that make you an adept investor or financial advisor.

If this is your unique ability, you have moments of clarity that are astounding. As you converse with others, the next course of action becomes crystal clear. You can see the issues, the obstacles, and the way to navigate the course ahead. The path is so clear to you that you can confidently lead people through. You may even become impatient with those who question your conclusions because the solution is just so clear to you.

> Some of you can see the issues, the obstacles, and the way to navigate the course ahead.

You can encourage a spouse who has unique wisdom through the following actions:

- Compliment your spouse's wisdom.

- Provide time for your spouse to interact with people who would benefit from her wisdom.

- Encourage your spouse to increase his knowledge in his area of expertise.

- Set aside time, money, or energy to be a team player in your spouse's learning adventure.

You will discourage a spouse who has unique wisdom through the following actions:

- Complain about how much time your spouse spends with other people.

- Point out that you think other people are more important to your spouse than you are.

- In public settings, share strong opinions in your spouse's area of expertise, rather than defer to him.

- Undercut your spouse's desire to learn and to grow in wisdom or to use her wisdom.

Category 3: Technology

We live in a highly technological age. It is hard to believe that so much of our life is controlled by very fast moving ones and zeros! Our lives are enhanced by computers, cell phones, portable media players, digital cable, global positioning devices, and home entertainment systems. The pace of growth in technology is so fast, however, that we can only imagine the technological wonders the future will hold for us. In the midst of relentless electronic development, some of you have been given unusual understanding into how all of this works. Computers are straightforward for you. The interconnection between computer networks, cell phones, and portable devices makes sense to you. When new technology appears, it doesn't take you long to figure it out and put it into action.

Some of you have a high aptitude for programming as well as

setting up and troubleshooting devices. We are all grateful to you for providing the rest of us with the technological advances we count on. Most of us could never do what you do. It doesn't take long for us to be completely overwhelmed when you explain to us how technology works at its most basic level.

In the midst of relentless electronic development, some of you have been given unusual understanding into how all of this works.

Others of you are very good at helping others interface with technology. You accept that much of technology is a foreign language to a large number of people who need to use it in their work or personal lives. You are able to explain procedures to us in simple terms we can understand. You are helping to make complex computer systems user-friendly so they can have widespread applications.

You can encourage a spouse who has technological skill through the following actions:

- Compliment your spouse's ability to understand technology.

- Encourage reasonable investments in equipment.

- Encourage activities that help your spouse learn more about technology.

- Ask for help with your computer or phone.

- Attend events with your spouse where technologies are introduced or marketed.

You will discourage a spouse who has technological skill through the following actions:

- Complain about how much time your spouse spends on the computer.

- Complain about how much electronic stuff costs.

- Whine about technology cluttering your life or making the world too complex.

- Act disinterested or apathetic toward technology

Category 4: Relationships

Many of you have strong natural instincts for the way relationships work. You sense people's moods and needs. You can predict how much time people need, and you creatively come up with ways to communicate that encourage and inspire others.

Some of you have relationship skills for the everyday interaction of friendship. You are good at staying in touch with people through e-mail, text messages, and phone conversations. You know what is happening in people's lives, and you regularly encourage them in their pursuits.

Others of you are talented in coaching others in their relationships. It probably began in your teen years when you noticed that your friends consistently came to you for advice in their relationships. You didn't really understand why they came to you, but you seemed to have answers for them. As an adult, you have been helping people figure out their relationships in a combination of casual and formal settings. Your friends probably call you for advice. You may be leading a Bible study or prayer group that focuses on the important relationships in one another's lives.

> Many of you have strong natural instincts for the way relationships work.

Some of you with this ability are helping others heal. You are probably a people helper by profession or you help lead a recovery ministry in your community. As others share their stories, you have an uncanny ability to see the path that will lead them away from their pain toward healthy decisions. You get burdened with the number of painful stories you hear, but you cannot escape the insight you have into the process that promotes healing in people's hearts.

You can encourage a spouse who is adept with relationships through the following actions:

- Compliment your spouse's ability to understand people.
- Tell your spouse that you are glad to be her friend.
- Provide ways for your spouse to stay in touch with people.
- Help your spouse establish healthy boundaries to prevent an overwhelming flow of conversations.

- Share some of your vacation time with family and friends.

You will discourage a spouse who is adept with relationships through the following actions:

- Complain about how often your spouse connects with others.

- Ignore your spouse's need to set up boundaries to keep this gift in line.

- Remove your spouse's ability to connect with people.

- Pile up your spouse with tasks so there is no time left for people.

Bill has this gift. I am constantly amazed how he can zero in on a person's real issue in discussions, how he can make perfect strangers feel at home with him in just minutes, and how he is always the life of the dinner party with his humorous stories and insightful questions.

Bill is so good with people. We might be in a group walking down any street in any city, and the homeless person begging for money or the mom who needs a jump start or a tire change will always ask Bill. Not me, not the other nine people we are with, always Bill! Bill often asks, "Why me? Why do they always pick me?" I tease him that it's because his Superman cape is sticking out from under his shirt.

Our son Zachery also has this gift. In college, Zach was the captain of his coed cheer team. Over a hundred peers looked to him for leadership and guidance, not only in the sport but also in their personal lives. His knack for helping friends think through their lives became so well known, even cheerleaders from other colleges would call on him for wisdom and guidance. We nicknamed him "Chaplain to the cheer world."

Because both Bill and Zach are so gifted with people, their lives can easily become a blur of people and those people's needs a constant waterfall of demands for help. Bill and Zach often need backup when it comes to enforcing boundaries.

Once, when we traveled to Hawaii for a much-needed vacation and anniversary celebration, I bought Bill a T-shirt that read, "Witness Protection Program: You Don't Know Me."

It didn't work.

The first day in the bed-and-breakfast, what we did for a living came out in conversation. Consequently, Bill spent some of the vacation counseling and helping others. Honestly, I didn't mind because he still made *plenty* of time for me. Besides, using his giftedness makes Bill more fun to be around when we do have time alone because he is feeling really great about himself and how God is working through him to help others.

I encourage Bill by giving spontaneous freedom to exercise his people gift. Bill encourages me by placing boundaries around the exercise of his gift so I always know I am the priority person on his heart.

Zach had to cancel for a time the text messaging feature on his cell phone because his friends were addicted to the "Zach on Demand" accessory on their cell phones. By setting boundaries, he helped his friends learn vital decision-making skills.

It was my job in both cases to give Bill and Zach permission to set boundaries, then encourage them to enforce those boundaries when I saw stress rising in their lives.

Category 5: Musical Talent

Music is a powerful force in our lives. Music stirs the heart, ignites our emotions, and engages our imaginations. It has the ability to connect our thoughts, emotions, and actions to inspire us to better things.

Some of you have been gifted with musical talent for the benefit of the rest of us. Your ears are tuned so you can play and sing on key. Your voice is equipped to sing. Musical instruments make sense to you, and the study of music is fascinating to you. You may be gifted in playing or singing or composing. You may enjoy the stage or the solitude of a studio, but you love music and are good at expressing yourself in song.

You can encourage a spouse who has musical talent through the following actions:

- Compliment your spouse's ability to express himself musically.

- Invest in instruments and music or voice lessons.

- Encourage your spouse's involvement in musical activities (a band, choir, or other musical group).

You will discourage a spouse who has musical talent through the following actions:

- Complain about how irritating it is to listen to music practice.

- Keep your spouse so busy with other things that there is no time in the schedule for musical expression.

- Tell your spouse she spends too much time making music and not enough time with you and your family.

Category 6: Creative Arts

Creative expression is one of the great gifts of life. It has given rise to drama, fine art, movies, television, home décor, and graphic art. If you have this gift, life makes sense to you in a way the average person doesn't comprehend. You see shapes, colors, and concepts with unusual clarity and beauty. When you express yourself, other people experience "aha" moments. They look at your artwork and say, "That is incredible." They ask you to create a logo but can explain to you only how they want it to feel. When you give the feeling a shape, they say to you, "That is it! How did you come up with that?" You can't really

> Creative expression is one of the great gifts of life.

answer their question because the idea just occurred to you, and you knew it was right.

You can encourage a spouse who is gifted in the creative arts through the following actions:

- Compliment your spouse's ability to inspire others.
- Provide your spouse the opportunity to be involved in a creative pursuit.
- Invest in lessons or training to enhance your spouse's natural skill.
- Display your spouse's work

You will discourage a spouse who is gifted in the creative arts through the following actions:

- Complain about how expressive your spouse is.
- Criticize your spouse's creative expression.
- Load up responsibility so your spouse has little time to develop creativity.
- Pressure your spouse to share creativity before she is ready for the world to see her work.

Our youngest son, Caleb, is the artist of the family, and he has an incredible ability to persevere. He will work on a drawing for days until he is pleased with it. He will pursue his sports goals with undaunting tenacity. People who know him are impressed with what he is able to accomplish and ask him to lead, even though he does so quietly.

Michael and Cindy have a relationship to be admired in the area of supporting a creative spouse. Cindy is a gifted songwriter and vocalist. I (Pam) have seen Michael travel as a sound tech to support Cindy at retreats and other outreach events. He also watches their children so she can write and compose. Michael is Cindy's wind beneath her wings.

Have you ever noticed how many Grammy and CMT award

winners thank God and then their mate when accepting an award? It takes a spouse who is a fan to rise and succeed.

Category 7: Leadership

Some of you are natural born leaders. You seem to rise to leadership in everything you have ever been involved with. Your peers have

> Some of you are natural born leaders.

chosen you to lead since childhood. Your ideas are respected, and your directions are generally put into action. You have noticed that some people try to lead, but others do not follow. You, on the other hand, always have a following, even when you wish you could be left alone.

You can encourage a spouse who skillfully leads through the following actions:

- Follow your spouse's lead.
- Compliment the vision that your spouse expresses.
- Do things that make your spouse's plan work more smoothly.
- Let others around your spouse know you value him as a leader.

You will discourage a spouse who skillfully leads through the following actions:

- Complain about most decisions that your spouse makes.
- Refuse to follow your spouse.
- Resist your spouse's efforts to make a difference.
- Be selfish with resources that, if you shared, could help your spouse accomplish goals.

Pam has this skill set. Decision-making is natural for her. She has written books such as *Woman of Influence, Woman of Confidence,* and *The 10 Best Decisions a Woman Can Make* because setting the pace for women is in her soul. Her love for ministering to couples and families grows out of her love to help women succeed in their most vital relationships. Because she is a visionary, a leader, a decision-maker, however, she needs a spouse who can flex and adapt as she changes course, sets plans in place, and moves through life at a frenetic pace. She needs a team around her to follow up and follow through on the plans she sets in motion.

I (Pam) often say it takes a strong man to marry a strong woman. Bill leads our family and our life, and one of the strengths of a good leader is to delegate. He has been my cheerleader and biggest supporter. Many of the women who are Christian speakers and leaders have husbands who see value in releasing their wives to use their God-given gifts.

Our oldest son, Brock, also has a unique ability to lead groups in competitive settings. The steps to success are clear to him, and he can confidently lead people to take those steps. As a result, he is naturally confident and thrives on challenges that require clear focus and intense effort. He is currently pursuing a football coaching career because it takes advantage of what he is best at.

Category 8: Communication

You may have unusual skill in communicating the principles of life to other people. Others listen to you and say, "Yeah, that's what I've been thinking but didn't know how to say it." You may prefer private conversations in which you share with friends your perspective on life or you may seek out opportunities to present in front of groups. You may be drawn to teaching as a profession or a hobby or you may be interested in public speaking. You may even discover that you have a knack for communication over public airwaves

> You may have unusual skill in communicating the principles of life to other people.

so that radio or television broadcasting is an attractive venture for you. In any case, you have a way with words that makes complex principles easy for the average person to digest.

You can encourage a spouse who communicates with skill through the following actions:

- Compliment your spouse's ability to explain the principles of life.
- Provide opportunities for your spouse to influence others.
- Seek out your spouse's advice often.

You will discourage a spouse who communicates with skill through the following actions:

- Complain about how many people your spouse interacts with.
- Accuse your spouse of being shallow or self-centered.
- Frequently cut your spouse off in conversation.

Category 9: Financial

In elementary school, you might have read about a mythological character named Midas—everything he touched turned to gold. Some of you have that touch. You love finances, and you are good at making and keeping money. You love the rush of making the deal or watching interest accumulate. A balanced Excel spreadsheet warms your heart.

> Some of you have the Midas touch. You love finances, and you are good at making and keeping money.

People with this gift often lead very busy lives. They may be corporate executives or entrepreneurs, but no matter the title, the hours can be long. The spouse married to a person with this Midas touch needs to value being married to someone God trusts enough to give money to as a steward.

You can encourage a spouse with the gift for finance through the following actions:

- Compliment your spouse's power to provide.
- Be independent enough to handle family and personal responsibilities (be low maintenance).

- Pray with your spouse on ways to use his gift to give generously to God's kingdom work or to train others to handle finances wisely and to work productively.

- Help your spouse launch a business.

You can discourage a spouse with the gift for finance through the following actions:

- Complain about how long your spouse works.

- Get jealous over whose paycheck is bigger.

- Refuse to attend social events that are a part of your spouse's career.

- Be a spendthrift.

Your affection for one another will grow when you value and appreciate the unique differences in each other and in each member of your family. Applaud the differences, delegate to the differences, and enjoy the differences. Make them work for you and for your family as you each seek to be the best for the team.

Decoder Moment: *Collect the Evidence:* So now it's time to get out the evidence bag and gather up the best clues to discern the strengths, gifts, talents, and skills you each possess. Mark the categories that apply to each member of your immediate family:

Unique Ability Category	Husband	Wife	Child 1	Child 2	Child 3	Child 4	Child 5
Physical Aptitudes							
Wisdom and Insight							
Technology							
Relationships							
Musical Talent							
Creative Arts							
Leadership							
Communication							
Financial							

Process the Evidence: It takes time and focus to determine your unique contribution to life. Each season of life offers more insight into who you were created to be. Each time you attempt to define your unique ability, it becomes a little clearer. Describe your unique ability as you understand it today. What are the best assets you can bring to the table?

Now list the traits and characteristics you most appreciate and value in your mate:

Take time to compliment each other and give specific examples of when your mate's strengths encouraged, blessed, or strengthened you.

The Key of Kindness

The key that unlocks the unique abilities in your marriage is kindness. We do not mean that you turn into overly nice people who never confront and never challenge one another. Kindness is the conclusion that we are all equal before God. Since we are equal, our talents have the same value as everyone else's in the family. If I believe that everyone in my family is as important as I am, I will be kind to them by putting as much effort into helping them grow and develop as I invest in my life. In this regard, Jesus is the kindest person who ever lived, and He set out the pattern for us in John 13:1-15:

> He now showed them the full extent of his love…he got up
> from the meal…and began to wash his disciples' feet…"Now

> that I, your Lord and Teacher, have washed your feet, you
> also should wash one another's feet. I have set you an exam-
> ple that you should do as I have done for you."

We have a relationship with Jesus because He is kind. We used to do things that war against a loving relationship. "At one time we too were foolish, disobedient, deceived and enslaved by all kinds of passions and pleasures. We lived in malice and envy, being hated and hating one another. But when the kindness and love of God our Savior appeared, he saved us" (Titus 3:3-5). In other words, an eternal relationship with Jesus was made possible by His kindness. He considered us as important as Himself and gave His life for us, and He has now passed the challenge on to us: "Do nothing out of selfish ambition or vain conceit, but in humility consider others better than yourselves. Each of you should look not only to your own interests, but also to the interests of others. Your attitude should be the same as that of Christ Jesus" (Philippians 2:3-5).

Kindness is a powerful tool. Consider all that kindness is able to do:

- It leads us to repentance (Romans 2:4).
- It leads to our adoption as sons and daughters of God (Ephesians 1:5).
- It gives us insight into the "mystery of God's will" (Ephesians 1:8-9).
- It connects us to forgiveness, which frees our hearts from bitterness (Colossians 3:12-13).
- It creates an atmosphere of growth (1 Peter 2:1-3).

THE POWER OF YOUR WORDS

Finally, one the best ways to express affection is through words. At the beginning of this century, John Gottman, a relationship researcher at the University of Washington, energized the entire field of marriage education with a conclusion that successful couples have five positive interactions for every one negative interaction.[9] We all knew by instinct that compliments and positive assurances were good for couples, but none of us had any empirical data to substantiate it.

We now know that couples who are determined to have secure and successful relationships will make positive interactions a common experience. Husbands will compliment their wives and wives will compliment their husbands often. They will compliment each other in the morning and at night. They will compliment each other face to face and through e-mail and cell phones. They will compliment each other's unique abilities and their attempts to grow. They will compliment each other when they are happy with one another and when they are in the midst of an argument. Positive statements about each other will become part of the atmosphere of their home.

We have developed some traditions in our interaction that keep the ratio high.

Pam: Every chance I get, I say to Bill, "You are such a good man." I often respond to his e-mails with, *I'm just no good without you.* I tell people when I know Bill can hear me, "He is the rudder that keeps my creativity focused. Without him, I would be all over the map."

Bill: Any time Pam says to me, "It's just me," I respond, "No, it's especially you." I often start e-mails to Pam with, *To my angel...*I remind Pam as often as I can, "I would have lived a much smaller life without you."

We both make it a habit to say, "I would rather be in this stressful situation with you than in an easy situation with anyone else." In the middle of business pursuits, we have leaned over to one another and whispered into each other's ears things we've said while we were making love.

We know this is all kind of corny, but it insures that the positive side of our relationship overwhelms the negative side of our relationship every week.

UNLOCKING THE CODE:
Dinner and Dialogue for a Heart-to-Heart Connection

Move your relationship "above the line" by completing the following statements:

"When I look at you, the unique strength I see is…"

"What I most appreciate about this strength is…"

Then ask:

"What can I do that encourages you in this area?"

"What is the kindest thing I have ever said? Done?"

"How does the way I touch you impact your area of strength and uniqueness?"

■■■

Our friend, Susan Wales, describes an "over the top" gift of kindness she gave one holiday:

> The summer after Ken and I were married, I wanted our first Christmas to be unforgettable…But a Christmas gift for my husband proved to be my greatest challenge thus far. As a longtime bachelor, Ken had bought for himself everything his heart desired—gadgets, the latest CD, volumes of books, and he had a stylish wardrobe in his closet, so what's a girl to do? He was in his fifties when we married, and I had recently turned forty, so there's not much you need at this age. December was fast approaching, and I still hadn't come up with a single idea.
>
> At the end of November, we were attending the last USC football game of the season and enjoying the halftime show when Ken told me how much he enjoyed watching the band, especially the baton twirlers. I smiled and told him proudly, "I was a majorette."
>
> He became so excited, and then he sighed wistfully, "Oh,

how I wish I had known you when you were young so I could have seen you twirl a baton. I always wanted to date a baton twirler."

Ah ha! I thought, *you will!*

We visited my parents at Christmas, and I went a few days earlier to help my mother with the preparations. When I picked Ken up at the Atlanta airport, he had no idea what I was wearing under my coat...Fortunately, I had not yet begun my middle-aged spread, so I could still squeeze into my high school uniform. En route to my parents' home, I pulled into the stadium.

"What?" Ken asked, confusion clouding his face. "Are we going to a ball game?"

"No, but you are about to get your Christmas gift...one you will never forget."

I flipped the switches, and the stadium lit up and the music came on. I plopped a tiara on my head, and my "halftime" show began. For the next hour, I twirled, twisted, tossed, danced, and jumped, as I performed to the marches of John Phillip Sousa and a variety of pop tunes to my audience of one.

Even after all these years, Ken still talks about our first Christmas and his unforgettable Christmas gift!

ABOVE THE LINE
_____
BELOW THE LINE

This e-mail is funny—but definitely not kind!

Eleven people—10 men and 1 woman—were hanging on a rope under a helicopter. The rope was not strong enough to carry them all, so they decided that one had to leave; otherwise they were all going to fall. They weren't able to choose that person, until the woman gave a very touching speech. She said that she would voluntarily let go of the rope because, as a woman, she was used to giving up everything for her husband and kids or for men in general. She was used to always making sacrifices with little in return. As soon as she finished her speech...*all the men started clapping.*

Chapter 4

Recreation

"The fruit of the Spirit is...patience..."

Our friend, Dawn Wilson, is one of the thousands who has caught the bug for geocaching, which is the high-tech game of treasure hunting.

"Geocaching has captured the imagination of more than a half-million adults in more than 200 countries," Dawn says. "Geocachers use a list of clues and a portable Global Positioning System (GPS) unit or GPS-enabled mobile phone to enter longitude and latitude coordinates from a Web site to find a cache, a hidden treasure.

"The game takes them through unfamiliar places, but at the end of the hunt is a trinket or toy, stashed in an airtight container, and a logbook to sign. It is usually easy to find the GPS coordinates, but locating the cache can be maddening. The terrain might be dangerous, and the hours of work, discouraging. Some caches have clues to *greater* caches, if the players are willing to do the work. The rules are simple. When you take something from the cache, leave something in the cache, and then write in the logbook. Finding the treasure is the goal, but the adventure is the real prize."

Dawn sees several parallels between geocaching and a healthy marriage.

"Marriage takes on a new dimension when the partners view their relationship as a treasure hunt! Each new discovery about one's partner is important, but the hunt itself brings joy and pleasure into the marriage.

"Studying your mate for clues about personal motivations and goals, strengths and weaknesses, and heartfelt needs brings not only knowledge, but excitement into your relationship. What you discover may be unfamiliar territory and, perhaps, not pleasant. The discovery process can be hard work, but it's worthwhile. Remember the geocachers! When you take, don't forget to give. Mutual, loving communication will help your relationship grow. Seek your mate's true heart, but don't forget to reveal your own."[10]

> "Marriage takes on a new dimension when the partners view their relationship as a treasure hunt!"
> —Dawn Wilson

Your Time Together

What's with men and their sports?

A man is getting married and is standing by his bride at the church. Also beside him are his golf clubs and bag.

His bride whispers, "What are your golf clubs doing here?"

And the man says, "This isn't going to take all day is it?"

What's up with women and all that shopping?

A woman was walking down the street when she was accosted by a dirty and shabby-looking homeless woman who asked her for a couple of dollars for dinner.

The woman took out her billfold, extracted ten dollars and asked, "If I give you this money, will you buy some wine with it instead of dinner?"

"No, I had to stop drinking years ago," the homeless woman replied.

"Will you use it to go shopping instead of buying food?"

"No, I don't waste time shopping. I need to spend all my time trying to stay alive."

"Will you spend this on a beauty salon instead of food?"

"Are you *nuts*! I haven't had my hair done in 20 years!"

"Well, I'm not going to give you the money," the woman said. "Instead, I'm going to take you out for dinner with my hubby and me tonight."

"Won't your hubby be furious with you for doing that? I know I'm dirty, and I probably smell pretty disgusting."

"That's okay. It's important for him to see what a woman looks like after she has given up shopping, hair appointments, and wine."

Somehow the jokes all seem to drift to couples spending less and less time together and more time apart doing things like golf and shopping. But is that really why we got married, for a tee time or a big holiday sale?

A Fun Friendship

"Successful couples have 'a mutual respect for and enjoyment of each other's company.'"[11] In other words, secure and successful couples make their friendship one of their highest priorities. They patiently invest time with each other and explore each other's hearts to build a life together.

It sounds simple, but it often goes against our instincts. When a woman builds a friendship with other women, she bases it on an exchange of ideas. She and her friends share their hopes, dreams, thoughts, and current experiences in a dynamic flow of ideas. They love to interact and talk about what is happening in their lives. They all approach life as an interconnected web of thoughts, emotions, and experiences so they naturally connect over words. Women consider a friendship secure when it is rich with conversation, vibrant with emotions, and full of dialogue.

Men, on the other hand, build friendship based on activities. They hunt together, fish together, work on computers together, build things together, make music together. While they do things side by side, they build camaraderie. Sometimes they share what is on their hearts with one another, and sometimes they just share the activity. Men consider a friendship successful when it is simple enough to make him feel capable or less stressed.

Since men and women approach friendship differently, what makes a friendship between a man and a woman flourish? A friendship between a husband and wife that builds an atmosphere of security and success has the following characteristics: They play together, they laugh together, they influence each other equally, they get to "know" each other, and they find their pace as a couple.

Play Together

You married each other because you liked each other's company, remember? You spent long hours talking, sharing your dreams, and exploring the desires in your hearts. You discovered a friendship that was unlike any you had ever experienced. There was acceptance, passion, encouragement, and fascination. Based on your compatibility, you decided to get married. Year after year you have added responsibilities, commitments, and financial obligations. Unless you have deliberately scheduled time for your love relationship, the duties of your life have taken over your schedule and your conversations. You have lots of discussions about bills, children, and time commitments but spend very little time talking about the hopes and dreams that make you a fascinating person.

Patience calms emotional resistance because love takes time.

Of course, you need to spend time talking about the responsibilities of your life. In order for your marriage to flourish, however, you need to have a significant amount of time together where you continue to knit your hearts together. This is more challenging during highly productive seasons of life because romantic attraction is inefficient. It doesn't work very well to say to your mate, "How are you feeling today? Can you tell me quickly because I have to get back to work?" This kind of a hurried pace to communication tends to close off the heart and create distance between an otherwise loving couple.

Your spouse will avoid opening up to you because he or she feels rushed. It will appear that life's responsibilities are more important to you than your spouse so he or she will automatically take a defensive posture with you. Patience calms emotional resistance because love takes time.

The time you spend dating your spouse is not an optional activity in your relationship. It is one of the prime activities that gives you energy for everything else in your life. Couples who experience their love regularly spend less time and energy in conflict with one another. Couples who are romantically connected are more confident and, thereby, more effective in their work pursuits. Couples who respect and admire one another tend to agree in the messages they give to their kids, which minimizes conflicts with children. As a result, romantic connection raises the energy level in your lives.

EVIDENCE COLLECTION:

Mark your answers to the following questions.

Husband:

I would like us to have a date
☐ once a week
☐ every other week
☐ once a month.

I like it better when we
☐ date on the same day of the week each time
☐ discuss what day we go out each time we plan a date.

I like our dates best when
☐ we go out
☐ we stay home.

I like our dates best when
☐ I plan the date
☐ my wife plans the date

☐ we take turns planning our dates
☐ we plan our dates together.

I like our dates to include
☐ just us
☐ another couple   ·
☐ a group.

I like our dates to include social time
☐ alone
☐ with people in our home
☐ with people outside our home.

Wife:

I would like us to have a date
☐ once a week
☐ every other week
☐ once a month.

I like it better when we
☐ date on the same day of the week each time
☐ discuss what day we go out each time we plan a date.

I like our dates best when
☐ we go out
☐ we stay home.

I like our dates best when
☐ I plan the date
☐ my husband plans the date
☐ we take turns planning our dates
☐ we plan our dates together.

I like our dates to include
☐ just us
☐ another couple
☐ a group.

I like our dates to include social time
☐ alone

☐ with people in our home
☐ with people outside our home.

Once you have marked your answers, get together and establish a dating routine as a couple. Choose how often you want to date and who will plan the dates. Our recommendation is that you spend time together weekly and take turns planning your time together, although one of you will probably plan more dates than the other.

When you meet together to talk about your dating routine, take time to mark the list below. Each of you mark as many of the activities as you enjoy. You can then use this list to help you plan your fun times together.

When we get to spend time together, I like it when we (add your own ideas in the blanks):

Activity	Husband	Wife
Casual Activities		
Share a meal together		
Watch a movie		
Attend a rodeo		
Shop		
Go to antique stores		
Go to concerts		
Visit museums		
Active Pursuits		
Take a walk in our neighborhood		
Hike a trail		
Canoe or kayak		
Boat, jet ski, water ski, or sail		
Bicycle		
Fly a kite		

Activity	Husband	Wife
Walk on the beach or around a lake		
Dance under the stars		
Snowboard, snow ski, or ride an inner tube on the snow		
Snowmobile		
Ride motorcycles or off-road vehicles		
Ride a horse		
Ride in a carriage, sleigh, or on a hay ride		
Snow sled or toboggan		
Inner tube down a river		
Bowl		
Jump rope, play hopscotch, or swing at the park		

Strenuous Pursuits

Activity	Husband	Wife
Rock climb		
Jog		
Work out at an athletic club (at the same time)		
Lift weights while we spot each other		
Jump on a trampoline		
Sky dive		
Participate in an aerobics or Pilates class		
Snorkel or scuba dive		
Wind surf		
Boogie board or surf		

Laugh Together

It is generally agreed that laughter is good for us. A good laugh will make you feel better physically and emotionally. Friends who laugh together love to be together. We committed early in our life together to make humor a priority. We carry plenty of pain in our life from childhood difficulties to adulthood disappointments. If we wanted to, we could drive ourselves crazy focusing on the negative side of life. In our experience, an intense focus on the negative things never makes them more positive. As a result, we decided to fill our life with reasons to laugh.

Practice laughing at yourself. Our imperfections create plenty of opportunities to be amused at our own behavior. As a young pastor, I (Bill) was trying to train our worship team to start the service with high energy. I sensed I wasn't communicating the concept well, so I decided to join the team for a few weeks and show them what I meant. I confidently stepped on the stage in front of the congregation and enthusiastically said, "Welcome to church this morning. Will you please stand and worship me!"

Of course I meant to say, "with me...worship with me," but I forgot a very important four letter word. I was just 29 years old, and I had been at this church for only three months, so I think they wondered if I really meant it. I knew I had said something wrong because they all had a look of shock on their faces. I stopped to think about what I had said and immediately started laughing. The shock on their faces changed to amusement, and they started laughing with me. I attempted to start the service several times, but I started to giggle every time I tried. We didn't get much done that morning, but it was one of the most memorable services we ever shared together.

One the best memories from our honeymoon was based on our inexperience. We celebrated the first week of our life together at a mountain resort in December. We were young, excited to be together, and thrilled with our very romantic hotel room. It had a king-sized bed and a beautiful rock fireplace. The first night, we opened the damper on the fireplace and built a glowing fire. We reveled in the romance. To me (Bill), Pam's beauty was further enhanced by the flicker of the flames. We had a wonderful time of making love and resting in each other's arms. We went to bed with the glimmering reflection of the fire dancing off the walls.

It never occurred to us that this might not be a good idea. The fire burned out sometime in the middle of the night, but the damper remained open. The heat from the furnace was sucked right up the chimney. When we got out from under the covers the next morning, we realized it was freezing in our room.

Pam grabbed the bedspread and ran across the room. I thought she wanted me to chase her around the room so we could warm up, so I jumped out of bed and ran after her. To my surprise, she stopped at the opposite side of the room, pulled the bedspread over her head, and put it against the wall around the furnace outlet. I slid under the spread with her so we could capture the warm air under our makeshift tent. We shivered together for a while before we thawed out, and then I ventured out just long enough to close the damper. After about two hours, we braved the 32 degree room to get dressed and headed to breakfast while the furnace attempted to deice the room.

We spent a week in Lake Tahoe, but the moment we remember the most is the morning spent huddled around the vent laughing about how our love had trapped us in a freezing room.

Collect jokes. We didn't want to rely just on our ability to find humor in the midst of life, so we started collecting jokes. Some are true stories, some come from audience members, others are sent to us, still others we find in joke books, the Sunday comics, or someplace on our quest for humor. Here's one of our favorites:

> A young boy sat down with his grandfather and said, "Grandpa, can I ask you a question?"
>
> "Sure, Donnie, what's on your mind?"
>
> "What do you call it when one person gets into bed on top of another person?"
>
> Grandpa grew a little nervous. He knew his grandson would become curious some day, and he wasn't sure if it was his place to talk to him about the facts of life. But he swallowed

hard and tentatively said, "Well, Donnie, that is called sexual intercourse."

Donnie nonchalantly responded, "Okay. Thanks Grandpa." He then gave him a hug and headed out the door.

About 15 minutes later, Donnie came back into his grandpa's room and said, "It is not, Grandpa. It's called bunk beds, and Mom wants to talk to you right now!"

When we find a joke we like, we type it up, save it in a computer file, and e-mail it to one another.

Stay alert to tension-breaking moments. We all experience moments in the midst of difficult situations that unexpectedly break the tension and cause us to break out in laughter…if we let them.

A couple approached us at one of our seminars with one of their favorite, true life stories. They had struggled for years with infertility. They longed to be parents and to raise a loving, healthy family. After years of trying, however, they found themselves agonizingly childless. They talked through their options and eventually decided upon artificial insemination. The husband would be the donor, and they would have a trusted doctor they knew perform the procedure.

As the date for the procedure drew close, the wife became increasingly melancholy. She was moping around the house, and her husband asked her, "Honey, what's wrong? We're getting ready to get pregnant. I thought you'd be excited."

"I am excited to become a mom, but I just feel it isn't supposed to be this way. Getting pregnant is intimate, and it's supposed to be passionate. I'm going into a doctor's office and just having a procedure. I just want it to be…special."

"I have an idea," her husband said. "I'll go into the doctor's office with you, and I'll sit by your head where I can whisper in your ear. At the very moment my sperm is inserted, I'll seductively sigh, 'Oh, baby. Oh, baby.' Do you think that will help?"

Through laughter, she told him he didn't have to do that, but that phrase has now become a great asset in their life. Whenever they face a tense moment, one of them will whisper to the other, "Oh, baby. Oh, baby." The laughter doesn't fix the situation, but it sure does set a great mood for working on it.

An Influential Friendship

Marriage is a partnership. You both have insight, wisdom, and expertise to offer. You have gained some form of education, you have significant life experiences, and you have instincts for certain aspects of life. If your friendship is strong, you will respect one another's contribution to life. You will listen to one another, learn from one another, defer to one another, and lead one another. You will naturally ask, "What advice do you have to add to this situation?"

This is generally a bigger struggle for men than for women. The part of a woman's brain that monitors verbal functioning is larger than the same area of a male brain. As a result, women explore more of life verbally and learn early the value of gathering various perspectives. They are much more comfortable considering different points of view and will change their opinions as new information becomes available.

Men, on the other hand, are driven to simplify things so they can easily succeed. They prefer to make decisions without a lot of deliberation, set up systems they follow on a regular basis, and avoid complicated discussions. The success of this part of the friendship is, therefore, more dependent on the husband than the wife, in most relationships.

This was a point of tension for us early in our marriage that has grown into a vital area of our friendship. When I (Bill) was working as a pastor in San Diego County, I would often open up to Pam about decisions I needed to make at church. I would describe my situation to her and ask her advice. Her response most often was, "Well, Bill, just do…" or "Why don't you simply do…" It didn't really matter what came next because those words set something off inside me that completely interrupted the conversation. I had already spent hours agonizing over the best course of action. Then, along came Pam with her "just do" and "it is simple" statements. It made me feel that either she was very insensitive or I was dense. Neither of those conclusions was very good for our friendship.

Along Came Pam

When I look at the big picture, however, I can't tell you how much I appreciate the way Pam has invested in my life. I was raised by an opinionated, creative, controlling, and fearful mom. She is incredibly talented, but the talent is hindered by fear. She is afraid to be involved with people, and she is afraid to express her creativity. Creative people need to express themselves or pressure builds up inside. My mom has enough creativity for a couple of lives, so you can imagine how intense the pressure was.

I never knew when my mom would be enthusiastic about life and when she would erupt in anger. Her fear caused her to control our environment to the point that we lived in isolation with no family friends and no social interaction outside of school and work. She protected the stronghold by insisting that we maintain the "family secret." We were not allowed to discuss what went on in our home with anyone except her. As a result, I developed a very private approach to life. I could simply have gone through my adult years isolated from any significant influence, which is a shame when you consider that my unique ability is helping people.

Then, along came Pam. She is also opinionated and creative. It has taken me a long time to be comfortable with this because you have heard that men tend to marry women like their moms. That was the single most frightening statement I had ever heard in my life! I thought I wanted to marry someone completely different than my mom because the stress of living with a fearful, controlling woman was unbearable. I have to admit, though, that I like opinions and I like creativity. The beauty of Pam is that she is the most fearless woman I have ever met. She believed in my talent long before I did. She has consistently identified opportunities for her talent, my talent, and the talents of each of our three boys to flourish. I, therefore, have lived a much bigger life than I ever dreamed possible when I was a young man.

Action on the Autobahn

We received an invitation in 2002 to travel to Germany to present a marriage conference for members of the army and their spouses. The troops had just returned from a tour in Iraq and were in the process of adjusting back to life at home. We got to be part of the integration team that helped in the transition. It was one of the most rewarding ventures we have been involved in.

We stayed at the home of Kevin, a career army veterinarian. His wife, Debbie, picked us up at the airport and drove us to their home at a leisurely 120 miles per hour on the autobahn. As we pulled up to the house, I noticed a bright red Mini Cooper in the driveway.

We had dinner with the family that evening, and I (Bill) casually said to Kevin, "Hey, I notice you have a Mini in the driveway. When are we going out on the Autobahn in that?"

His eighteen-year-old son blurted out, "I'll take you out. It'll be fun!"

Me and my big mouth. I had just traveled across the Atlantic Ocean to encourage soldiers and their wives, and I was about to put my life in the hands of a teenage driver! Though I knew this was not a wise idea, I wasn't about to show an eighteen-year-old that I was afraid.

As soon as dinner was finished, my adolescent chauffer said, "So, are you ready?"

"Yeah, let's hit it," I said enthusiastically.

I wasn't too nervous until Debbie said to her son, "No going over 130 since it's his first time."

We cruised through the city streets and then took the onramp to the right. He shifted, mashed down the accelerator, and the Mini shot me back in my seat as I sent up a desperate prayer for protection.

We sped down the autobahn in impressive fashion. I heard the tires squeal only once. I noticed he drove 129.9 miles per hour but, to his credit, he never went over 130. It was one of the great guy memories of my life.

I'm convinced that I would never have had that experience were I not married to Pam. A fearful woman wouldn't have traveled to Germany alone the first time to speak to Army wives and lay the foundation for us to return. A fearful woman wouldn't have let her husband step foot in a Mini Cooper driven on the autobahn by anyone, especially not a teenager. But Pam believes in a big God and His ability to control all of life's details. As a result, fear does not determine her decisions. She honestly believes the whole world ought to hear what God has done in our lives and what He has taught us along the journey, and if traveling to foreign countries, hiking trails, navigating rivers, or dealing with armed guards are a part of the journey God has for us, then she will say "Yes!" She even says, "Yes" to a little fun in a Mini Cooper along the way. Her investment in my life has energized my unique ability beyond anything I ever dreamed of.

Getting to Know You

When it comes to knowing your spouse, John Gottman in *The Seven Principles for Making Marriage Work* includes the following questions to help you assess how well you know each other.

Answer each of these true or false:

T F   I can name my partner's best friends.

T F   I know what stresses my partner currently faces.

T F   I know the names of those who have been irritating my partner lately.

T F   I know some of my partner's life dreams.

T F   I am very familiar with my partner's religious beliefs.

T F   I can outline my partner's basic philosophy of life.

T F   I can list the relatives my partner likes least.

T F   I know my partner's favorite music.

T F   I can list my partner's favorite three movies.

T F   I know the most stressful thing that happened to my partner in childhood.

T F   I can list my partner's major aspirations.

T F   I know what my partner would do if he/she won the lottery.

T F   I can relate in detail my first impressions of my partner.

T F   I ask my partner about his/her world periodically.

T F   I feel my partner knows me fairly well.

__ __   Total number of T/F out of 15

SCORING: If you answered true to more than half, this is an area of strength in your marriage.[12] If you do not know the answer to at least half the questions, get together once a week for the next few weeks specifically to discuss these. Choose one of the questions per week and take turns sharing your thoughts with one another. Be patient with one another and don't let these become problem-solving sessions where you ask each other a lot of "why" questions. Spend this time with each other just being curious about one another.

Finding Your Pace

Sometimes, you learn the most important lessons of life at unexpected times. Pam and I were organizing a bicycle trip for a group of teenagers. We were all inexperienced so we asked a professional bike rider to train us for the trip. In one of the sessions, he made the following observation:

> You have gears on your bicycle so that you can stay at your pace. When you ride for long distances, it's important that you find the pace at which your feet go around most comfortably. You all have a pace that you can maintain all day long. As you ride, look for your comfortable pace and change the gears on your bike so that your feet go at that pace. If you go faster than your pace, you will fatigue yourself. If you go slower than your pace, you will also fatigue yourself. The key is to go at your pace.

Your pace is a combination of the speed at which you like to live, the magnitude of your goals, and the level of influence you want to maintain. If you like to move quickly, have big goals, and want to influence a large number of people, your pace will be faster. If you like to move slowly, prefer smaller goals, or prefer to go deep as you influence a limited number of people, your pace will be slower. The people you want to influence will affect the pace too. If you want to impact youth, children, or those chasing their dreams, you will need to run at a quicker clip. If you want to leave an imprint on babies or the more mature seniors, however, you can slow down some and move at a pace they are more comfortable with.

Whether your pace is fast or slow, you are still moving, you have goals, and you are influencing others. Therefore, the value of your pace is not determined by its swiftness. People of all paces are valuable in society. Your pace is valuable because it is your pace. You can run at this rate all day everyday without getting fatigued. If you try to live faster or slower, you will find yourself exhausted and overwhelmed.

As an individual, you have a pace of life you enjoy. As a couple, you have a pace at which your relationship functions best.

For some couples, a dual career leaves little time for connection, so they prefer a more manageable model of one spouse at home or employed from home so they have more control of life's schedules and demands. For others, they both love to run at a quick pace, and the magic of romance seems to be the game of finding and creating time together. For other couples, they both prefer a more meandering stroll through life. One of you might prefer a faster pace than the other, so adjustments and compromises will help you create a pace of life in which you can both find happiness and contentment.

YOUR PACE AS AN INDIVIDUAL

Discovering your pace is one of life's great adventures. To help you discover your individual pace, collect evidence.

Evidence collection: Circle the answer that best finishes each statement for you as an individual. Use a different color for each of you.

1. I like to move (a) slowly (b) at a moderate speed (c) faster than most people (d) aggressively.

2. I like goals that are (a) easy to attain (b) like most people's goals (c) large (d) life changing.

3. In my lifetime, I want to influence (a) very few people (b) the people in my family and a few close friends (c) a significant number of people in my community (d) a large number of people in the world around me.

4. I like my life best when my pace is (a) slower than that of the average person (b) about the same as that of the average person (c) faster than that of the average person (d) unattainable by the average person.

5. Heaven to me is (a) the 24-hour life of the city (b) the steady hum of the suburbs (c) the gentle walk but hard work and consistency of the country (d) the quiet introspective stroll of life in the mountains, cabin, or on a quiet beach or lake, tucked away from the world.

Based on your answers, mark the statement that best describes your individual pace:

Husband:

☐ My pace is slower than that of the average person

☐ My pace is about the same as that of the average person

☐ My pace is faster than that of the average person

☐ My pace is aggressive and would be uncomfortable for the average person

Wife:

☐ My pace is slower than that of the average person

☐ My pace is about the same as that of the average person

☐ My pace is faster than that of the average person

☐ My pace is aggressive and would be uncomfortable for the average person

Your Pace as a Couple

If you were living your life in isolation, you could just run at your pace and enjoy your pursuits with complete control. However, God places us in relationships to promote growth we would not experience on our own. We all get married because we want someone to love us, encourage us, and romance us. It doesn't take long until we figure out that much of marriage is defined by Proverbs 27:17, "As iron sharpens iron, so one man sharpens another." We wanted a relationship that was smooth and easy and found it to be sharp and demanding.

You can no longer run just at your pace; you now need to figure out your pace as a couple. If your pace as a couple is similar to your individual pace, you love it. If your pace as a couple is more like your spouse's, you will fear that you are being left out as you are forced to live

If your pace as a couple is similar to your individual pace, you love it.

a pace you are not comfortable with. The fear can be softened if you take time to pursue your pace together. No hard and fast formula exists for identifying your pace, so you must be patient. It takes time, discussions, adjustments, and curiosity to discover the pace that works best for you as husband and wife. To help you figure out your relationship pace, collect evidence:

EVIDENCE COLLECTION:

Circle the answer that best finishes each statement for you as a couple.

1. We like to move (a) slowly (b) at a moderate speed (c) faster than most couples (d) aggressively.

2. We like goals that are (a) easy to attain (b) like most couples' goals (c) large (d) life changing.

3. In our lifetime, we want to influence (a) very few people (b) the people in our families and a few close friends (c) a significant number of people in our community (d) a large number of people in the world around us.

4. We like our life best when our pace is (a) slower than that of the average couple (b) about the same as that of the average couple (c) faster than that of the average couple (d) unattainable by the average couple.

Based on your answers, mark the statement that best describes your pace as a couple:

☐ Our pace is slower than that of the average couple

☐ Our pace is about the same as that of the average couple

☐ Our pace is faster than that of the average couple

☐ Our pace is aggressive and would be uncomfortable for the average couple

Once you identify your pace, practice asking the following question when you as a couple are faced with a decision: "Will this decision help us live at our pace?"

 **UNLOCKING THE CODE:**
Dinner and Dialogue for a Heart-to-Heart Connection

Each of you share what a "real day off" might look like. Lay out a 24-hour plan and share why it's a day you would enjoy. After you both share, select a weekend where each of you gets to live out your 24-hour plan. You might have to adapt your plans to match the funds available or your specific schedule, but place the weekend on the calendar so you have something to look forward to.

■ ■ ■

The day before Thanksgiving, a man in Ohio called his adult son in Michigan. "Son, I've had enough. After 40 years of marriage, I've decided to leave your mother."

The son hysterically responded, "Dad, this cannot be happening. Don't do a thing until we get there to talk some sense into you!"

The son then called his sister in Illinois who became equally hysterical. She also called her father: "Dad, we're not going to let this happen. You and Mom stay put. We'll be there tomorrow to work things out!"

The father hung up the phone and said to his wife, "The kids are coming for Thanksgiving, and they're paying their own way."

ABOVE THE LINE
_____
BELOW THE LINE

A little boy attended his first wedding. His cousin asked him, "How many women can a man marry?"

"Sixteen," the boy responded.

His cousin, amazed that he had an answer so quickly, said, "How do you know that?"

"Easy. All you have to do is add it up like the pastor said—'four better, four worse, four richer, four poorer.'"

Chapter 5

Resolving Conflicts

"The fruit of the Spirit is...peace..."

Conflict is an ordinary part of every intimate relationship. We all entertain the thought that we should be able to get along with this person who has captured our heart because there is something special between us. While this is true most of the time, it is nearly impossible to connect your life to another individual and not have significant disagreements. As you go through your journey together, you will get under each other's skin and challenge each other to search the depths of your heart for what really matters to you.

Conflict, however, can be resolved so that it brings value to your relationship. Conflict always feels bad when it starts, but if you handle it well as a couple, it will bring value and appreciation to your marriage. You will be reminded that you have passion for this relationship. You will be reminded that some issues are important enough for you to care about at a very deep level. You will be reminded that you make a difference in each other's lives.

Before we talk about how to handle conflict, let's look at the reasons why every intimate relationship experiences tension. A number of triggers bring conflict to the surface of your relationship.

I Don't Want to Look Stupid!

You are very aware of the inconsistencies within yourself because you live with them every day. You have learned to compensate for them, but you work hard to keep them under wraps. When they get exposed by the actions of your spouse, they make you feel vulnerable and insecure. If they rise to the surface while you are in a social setting and your spouse responds insensitively, you will feel doubly vulnerable. We think the problem is with the other person but, in reality, he or she is just the mirror that exposes the inconsistencies in each of us. You want to be a good spouse, but you are afraid you may not have what it takes to meet your spouse's needs. You want to be productive enough to provide for your family, but you are afraid your work may not be good enough. You want to have great relationships, but you are all too aware of the things you say and do that make you feel inadequate. You are afraid of being "that guy" or "that woman" who looks or sounds silly.

> You are very aware of the inconsistencies within yourself because you live with them every day.

Because your spouse is closer to you than anyone else, his or her opinion of you (or perceived opinion of you) has the ability to raise more pleasure and more irritation than anyone else's opinion on earth.

I Am Bored

Some of the conflicts in your marriage happen because boredom sets in. You are not necessarily upset with each other, there just isn't much enthusiasm. Consider Mike and Myra Modern. They met each other through an online service. They loved this approach because the surveys they filled out and the diagnostic tools they utilized helped them define themselves and what they were looking for in a mate. Their answers seemed so similar that an instant attraction took place just from reading about each another. As they exchanged e-mails, the attraction continued to grow. They were both amazed at the similarities in their e-mail styles, the consistency of their preferences, and how in sync their convictions appeared to be.

After a few months without a hitch, they decided it was time to meet face to face. Mike flew to Myra's hometown for a hopeful (although fearful) encounter. Just like everything else in their relationship, the weekend went extremely well. The attraction was instantaneous and intense. They both knew after this first face-to-face encounter that this was the one. Within three more months they were engaged, and they exchanged their wedding vows about a year after their first e-mail conversation.

With this kind of magical beginning, Mike and Myra believed they would experience an incredibly satisfying marriage. They anticipated smooth decision-making since they were so in tune with each other. They never said it out loud, but they expected they would have a near perfect relationship. After all, they were attracted to one another because they were so much like each other.

Reality Is a Little Different

Reality was a little different from Mike and Myra's hopes and aspirations. Mike is an introvert energized by time alone. When free time is available, he prefers to be left alone to exercise or work on the yard or play with his electronic gadgets. Myra is an extrovert energized by people. When free time is available, she prefers to seek out a social setting where she can engage in stimulating conversation and share stories about life. This is not a big problem, but they get frustrated with each other almost every time there is free time. Mike is afraid to give in to Myra because he feels he will be used up by constant social interaction. Myra is afraid to give in to Mike because she is afraid she will be bored for the rest of their lives.

Additionally, Mike and Myra are committed to their careers. They are professionals who have worked hard to attain a position of influence and security. They are both willing to do what it takes to succeed in their chosen paths. Both of them often work late and have to respond spontaneously to challenges that arise.

Synchronizing their schedules is one of their biggest struggles. Mike is surprised by the anger that arises in his heart when Myra asks him to adjust his schedule to the demands of her schedule. He knows he should not respond this intensely to the woman he loves, but the fear that he cannot take care of his career jumps on him quickly and seems relentless.

Myra is surprised by how offended she gets when Mike asks her to adjust to his schedule. She thinks she should probably trust him more, but her thoughts and emotions ignite so quickly, she seems powerless to think through the issue. She is afraid that Mike will squelch her career to get his needs met.

They can't seem to find a solution to this, so they do their best to ignore the undercurrent of irritation. They don't talk about it much anymore. Instead, they silently protect their schedules and hope it will be better someday.

Life between the two of them has become pragmatic. They do well talking about household responsibilities and the events of the week. They have their financial house in order. They have clearly defined responsibilities at home, and they take a yearly vacation. To their disappointment, their communication has also become pragmatic. They don't feel free to be vulnerable and to talk about their hopes and dreams, their disappointments and inconsistencies. They put up a good front with each other so they can function well, but they both miss the intimacy they believed would come easily in their relationship. They are not sure how it developed, but they now keep things on a shallow level. They are strangely afraid that they will fail with each other if they become too vulnerable.

They are not upset with each other, they are just bored. The magical, exciting relationship that seemed so easy to achieve when they were dating has disappeared, and they don't understand why or how it happened.

If you don't believe that you are being taken care of, you will guard your life and make demands that the ones you love take care of you. You will no longer be able to serve or to give yourself sacrificially to the ones who need you most. Brick by brick, this self-protection mode will build a wall between you.

Decoder Moment: Break the boredom! Each of you answer this question: What is one idea you'd like to try, place you'd like to go, or experience you'd like to have that is outside your comfort zone (but not immoral or illegal)?

Triggers from the Past

Another reason conflict exists in the typical marriage is that we sometimes trigger painful reactions from the past in each other. They may be tied to experiences during your childhood or to experiences from earlier in your adulthood. Either way, they get set off by something your spouse says or does that brings up the pain. These conflicts tend to be a little weird because they are reactions to a past event rather than the events of today. You suddenly don't feel safe, and you go into action to protect yourself. When you feel danger is imminent, you will use logic, outbursts, unreasonable behavior, anger, and any other tactic that will make you feel like you are out of danger.

I (Bill) spent time with my parents while writing this book. My dad has some serious physical challenges from a stroke he experienced in his forties, and I was at their house to take him to a doctor's appointment. My dad is slow and awkward, but he is very capable of taking care of himself. He dresses himself, walks with a cane, and can get himself in and out of the car. My mom, however, hovers over him like heavy fog. She is afraid that my dad needs help and that he will hurt himself unless someone sticks close to him. I accept that this is important to my mom and that it is her choice to live this way.

I am amazed, however, at how upset I get when she tries to pass her fears on to me. She got it in her mind that I needed to practice helping my dad get in and out of the car and walk him from the car to a building. I know that my dad does not need this kind of help. And even if he did, I think I have the capacity to help Dad without practicing in this way. My dad, on the other hand, has decided to just go along with my mom's whims.

We decided to go to a restaurant for our practice session and got there before it opened, so I parked in a shaded parking space to wait. My plan was to move the car to a handicap space as soon as the restaurant opened, and then do our "practice session." I tried to explain that to my mom, but she overran my suggestion and pushed hard for her agenda. My dad said we would go along with her plan.

My blood went to instant boil. My anger shot to every nerve in my body. My muscles tensed, my thoughts went wild, and my adrenaline surged. In very mature fashion, I got out of the car and slammed the door!

I am generally a peaceful, easygoing man, but I apparently have a big red button that my mom has access to. I have worked hard to forgive her for the things she has done, the things she has said, and the negative influence she has had on my life. The process is ongoing.

Fortunately, my mom's funky behavior today does not usher in the wave of past hurt like it used to. This time, the sting in my mom's demands didn't last long. I recognized the response I needed to select, so I stopped myself right after I slammed the door and stood next to the car for a moment. I said to myself, *Don't let her do it! She used to make you mad every time you saw her. You even stopped seeing your dad for a while because she was too hard to be around. You don't need to let her win. Take a breath. Calm down. Look at the humor. A small woman with a long list of fears is getting under the skin of a person who is writing a book about overcoming fear. Your dad faced huge challenges to help get men on the moon, but he doesn't know what to do with his wife. It won't hurt anyone or anything to go along with her fear-riddled scheme. You don't have to be sucked into fear's vortex even if you let your mom have her way on this benign request. You can return home tonight, to a home centered on joy not fear, and get back to a normal life. This won't last long, and she no longer has control of your life.*

She Is Not My Mom, But...

I would love to tell you that I never project these reactions onto Pam, but you would know it is not true. I have worked hard to put my mom's negative influence behind me, but there are a few reactions in my life that appear to be lifelong struggles. There are few things on earth that can stir me up as much as a woman who does not make sense to me. This puts a lot of pressure on Pam to be logical and consistent in her thinking. Intellectually, I know this is not fair to her, so I choose to keep on the slow but steady growth tract.

Not far behind the "she doesn't make sense" reaction is the "I was left out of an important decision" reaction. My mom aggressively controlled most of the decisions in our family in an attempt to calm her fears. I remember thinking that it didn't matter what I thought about anything because it would just be overrun by my mom's need to control. As an adult, I was determined to not allow others to make important decisions for me. Well, Pam is a great decision-maker. I was attracted to her because she was strong and stated her opinions with skill. I know it would not be fair to force her to check in with me before she makes decisions, so there are times when I fight resentment over decisions she has made that I think I should have been given an equal say in.

These are responses I brought with me to the marriage. They reside inside me and come to the surface when they are triggered by Pam's actions. It is easy to blame Pam for these because she is the one who brings them to the surface, but she does not cause them. Even if she were to change, the reaction would still reside in me waiting to be triggered by some stimulus.

Decoder Moment: Each of you share one incident from your past (before your wedding day) that still triggers emotions in your marriage. Describe what happened in the past and when you feel those emotions well up today. You don't need to problem solve, simply express your appreciation that your mate shared this deep personal emotion with you.

Honest Disagreements

One of the most common reasons you argue is that you honestly disagree with each other over some decision that is important to both of you. It may involve your kids, your finances, or your schedule. It is awesome when you agree because it feels like you are on the same team working on the same goals. It is agonizing when you disagree because this is your partner in life and these decisions involve the things that are most dear to your heart.

A man was asked what the secret was to his 50 years of harmonious marriage. He said, "When my wife and I first got married, we agreed that she would make all the minor decisions and I would make all the major decisions. To date, there have been no major decisions."

Pam and I were at a car dealership committing to our first minivan. Our family had grown to five, and we needed a functional family vehicle. We found the vehicle we wanted and were escorted to an office where we could talk options. My approach was to take things carefully and to not overbuy. We agreed ahead of time that I would be in charge of the negotiation.

> You are highly influenced by your spouse—that is why you married him or her and that is why you experience conflict.

The lady who was helping us started showing us options for the minivan. "We can put an alarm system on the vehicle that will lock and unlock the doors with a remote. You can also push a button and locate your van in a crowded parking lot if you forgot where you parked."

Pam blurted out, "Oh, that's great. I want that."

So much for negotiating! It was a frustrating moment because I thought I was going to make the decision, but in the enthusiasm of the moment, Pam ended up taking charge.

Afterward, we rejoiced over the purchase of our new vehicle and argued over the process of how it went down. I felt a need to express my frustration, even though I knew there wasn't any real solution. I just needed to get to a point where I appreciated Pam's spontaneity and enthusiasm once again. (And the next time we purchased a car, Pam said, "Bill, I love you, I trust you. This is the type of vehicle I think I'd like, so something in that ballpark is great. But this time, for the sake of our checkbook, I'm staying home and letting you do the negotiating!")

Pam and I had a hard time working through the purchase of a truck for one of our sons. This particular son has a personality similar to Pam's, so she has intense instincts regarding his needs. As you may have figured out, my role in the family is to remind everyone that we need to exercise caution as we ambitiously pursue our goals. This set the scene for a very tense discussion.

"I think we should convince our son to buy a smaller truck that gets better gas mileage," I stated with conviction. "He will have this truck all through college and probably in the early years of his marriage. Lower gas mileage would be a good thing."

"I know that, but he has had a hard year and he's discouraged," Pam said. "He's attached to the idea that he will get this truck. I know that he will be disillusioned if we don't do this for him."

"You mean his emotional needs are more important than financial logic?" I asked, thinking this would convince Pam to follow my lead.

"This is about his motivation. If he gets disillusioned, he won't perform well in college. If his grades are bad in college, he won't succeed in his career, and I don't think I can live with that," Pam said with equal conviction.

We had this same conversation in many versions to no avail. We finally had to schedule a lengthy meeting with each other where we wrote down all our thoughts about the purchase. We then took the list and prioritized our thoughts. The highly important ones received an A priority. The sort of important ones received a B. The thoughts we came up with because we are creative received a C. At that meeting, we finally came to the conclusion that our son's motivation and ability to carry team equipment (he was joining a competitive college team) were the most important factors. Based on that, we committed to the larger truck. Our son was excited, to say the least!

Your Highly Influential Spouse

You are highly influenced by your spouse—that is why you married him or her and that is why you experience conflict. You are more inspired by your mate than by anyone else on earth. At the same time, you get more frustrated with your spouse than with anyone else on earth. Both of these reactions happen because you have opened up your heart and have become vulnerable to each other. The fear develops along a subtle path:

1. You are fascinated with the way your spouse approaches life. If you are a Peacekeeper, you are amazed at how Decision-Makers can move forward with such authority. If you are an Inspirer, you are amazed at how organized the Policyholder is, and so on.

2. You choose to trust some area of life to your spouse and vow to follow his or her lead in this area.

3. You share your opinion with your spouse in this area he or she is responsible for. Since it is your opinion, you think it is a pretty good idea.

4. Your idea is dismissed by your spouse because it does not line up with his or her style.

5. You start to wonder if your opinion matters to your spouse.

6. The thought that your perspective will not be included by your spouse turns into a fear that you will be left out of the decisions he or she will make in the future.

7. Left unresolved, the fear erodes trust between you and your spouse as you protect your ability to be included in the decisions of life you consider important.

SUCCESSFUL CONFLICTS

Take Responsibility

The first step in resolving conflict is to *take responsibility for your side of the relationship*. Decide what *you* will do since this is all you have control over. If you focus on changing your spouse to make you feel safe, you will throw your emotions and thoughts out of control. You will place your well-being in the hands of the one you love. Your mate may love you immensely, but he or she is not capable of erasing the issues because they reside within you. Only you can take responsibility for the concerns that keep you from being able to love.

Once your reactions are under your control, you will interpret your spouse's responses back to you in a much different way. Rather than see them as a threat, you will see them as an expression of your spouse's insecurities and needs. You will be able to work on your growth while you trust God to work on the growth of your spouse. When your reactions to your spouse are free of fear, the relationship grows from your side. If the responses you get back are free of fear, you will effectively turn conflict into another reminder of just how in love you are.

> The first step in resolving conflict is to take personal responsibility for your side of the relationship. If you focus on changing your spouse to make you feel safe, you will throw your emotions and thoughts out of control.

Let's just own the fact we are not perfect. We do our best to carry the following thought in our hearts into our disagreements. We imagine God saying to us, "I am God, so I am in control. I have your best interests on My heart and mind. I love you, so you can choose joy and be free to love again. No need to protect your territory, I am protecting your heart and life so you can love!"

Be Patient

The second step to resolving conflict is *patience*. If you believe your opinion does not matter to your spouse or you sense that life will change without your permission, you will be tempted to take things into your own hands rather than wait for God to direct your life and your marriage. As an individual, patience is the willingness to wait to see what God is going to do in my life. As a spouse, patience is the commitment to work on my growth while I wait for God to make whatever changes He thinks are necessary in my spouse.

You have entered a long-term relationship that is not dependent on instantaneous resolution to all your issues. Some conflicts can be figured out quickly while others may take some time. You want to give the larger issues of your marriage the necessary time to work themselves out without panicking.

Some of the best things come to our life through waiting. Consider these statements from the Bible concerning the value of waiting:

- Waiting builds strength. Psalm 27 begins with a statement of courage based on a relationship with God, "The LORD is my light and my salvation—whom shall I fear? The LORD is the stronghold of my life—of whom shall I be afraid?" (v. 1) and ends with a commitment to wait, "I am still confident of this: I will see the goodness of the LORD in the land of the living. Wait for the LORD; be strong and take heart and wait for the LORD" (vv. 13-14).

- Waiting builds hope. "But the eyes of the LORD are on those who fear him, on those whose hope is in his unfailing love… We wait in hope for the LORD; he is our help and our shield. In him our hearts rejoice, for we trust in his holy name" (Psalm 33:18,20-21).

- Waiting prepares you for success. "Wait for the LORD and keep his way. He will exalt you to inherit the land…" (Psalm 37:34).

- Waiting trains you to listen to God. "I wait for you, O LORD; you will answer, O Lord my God" (Psalm 38:15).

- Waiting makes you more stable. "I waited patiently for the LORD…he set my feet on a rock and gave me a firm place to stand" (Psalm 40:1-2).

- Waiting moves you away from revenge. "Do not say, 'I'll pay you back for this wrong!' Wait for the LORD, and he will deliver you" (Proverbs 20:22).

- Waiting helps you experience God's compassion. "Yet the LORD longs to be gracious to you; he rises to show you compassion. For the LORD is a God of justice. Blessed are all who wait for him!" (Isaiah 30:18).

- Waiting protects you from being short-sighted. "Therefore

judge nothing before the appointed time; wait till the Lord comes. He will bring to light what is hidden in darkness and will expose the motives of men's hearts. At that time each will receive his praise from God" (1 Corinthians 4:5).

Waiting Is Active

A lot of people find waiting unattractive because they think it's a passive experience. We wait around doing nothing while we wait for God to do something. The good news is that waiting is an active pursuit. Consider the active steps that are a part of waiting in Psalm 37:

- Take care of current responsibilities (v. 3).
- Pursue an affectionate relationship with God (v. 4).
- Set goals, make a plan, and commit it to the Lord (v. 5).
- Pursue your purpose and fight against the tendency to compare your life to others (v. 7).

One of our favorite phone calls that illustrates the importance of taking care of current responsibilities was from a truck driver. The message went something like this:

> I was just callin' to thank ya'll for writing that book, *Men Are Like Waffles, Women Are Like Pasta.* I picked it up on I-90 at a truck stop. It's a good thing I did too. See, I have been bad.
>
> The good news is that waiting is an active pursuit.
>
> I have been a liar and a cheat, and before I left my ol' lady, she done kicked me out. Packed my bags and told me not to bother comin' home.
>
> But I picked up that book of yours and I read in it some stuff that made a whole lotta sense. I read the part about how you say if you give your heart to God, He can fix things.
>
> Well, I ain't never been to a church before, but I called up my ol' lady and I told her, "Darling, I have been bad and stupid.

What I did to you was flat out wrong, and I am begging your forgiveness. See honey, I picked up this here book because I heard the couple talking on the radio, and they said if we were to go to church, then maybe God would help us and we could start again. I know I don't deserve another chance, but I'm praying you will give me one."

Well, my darling wife told me I could come on home, and so I just called to tell ya thanks and we'll be in church on Sunday, so you be praying for us, will ya?

Waiting Gets You Ready

Waiting is one of life's most strategic skills because it prepares in us the character we need to accomplish our best feats and it positions us to be in the right place at the right time. Looking back, we are either glad we waited or we regret that we didn't wait.

In the midst of life, however, waiting seems to be torture. We get frustrated that we cannot make things happen faster, and we begin to feel we are victimized by life rather than living as conquerors. It is all too easy to reach the conclusion that nothing will happen, or the wrong thing will happen, if we don't jump in and do something about it.

In reality, waiting prepares each of us for our greatest moments. God knows when we have developed the character and skills necessary for the next venture, so He has us wait. We think we are ready sooner, so we get in a hurry. God knows when the circumstances of life are ready for our contribution, so He has us wait. We conclude that circumstances are moving too slow, so we get in a hurry. God knows how our actions react with everybody else's actions, so He has us wait. We are greatly concerned about the outcome of our lives, so we get in a hurry. But our impatience opposes what God is trying to do through us.

This is especially true in our marriages. You are intensely aware of the changes that need to take place in your life, but you are patient with yourself because you know that some things just take time to improve. You are also intensely aware of the changes that need to take place in your spouse, but you are impatient because your spouse's deficiencies interrupt your life. You want your spouse to change quickly so that your life can be how you want it to be. At the same time, you want your spouse to be patient with you so you can grow in a safe environment. The

> God knows when we have developed the character and skills necessary for the next venture, so He has us wait.

goal is to be as patient with your spouse as you are with yourself.

Choose a Plan

The final step in resolving conflict in your marriage is to *choose a plan you will follow as a couple*. When faced with a conflict in your marriage, choose one of the following approaches:

The Planned Approach

Schedule a time to meet to discuss what you are upset about. Your conflicts will almost always be highly emotional. Your spouse is the only person on earth with whom you share everything. Your finances, your emotions, your body, your social calendar, and your dreams are all attached to this person to whom you said, "I do." As a result, when you have a disagreement, intense emotions surface with the potential to take over the discussion. This is further complicated by the fact that men tend to get flooded by intense emotions and shut down in defense. When this happens, couples often struggle to reach any resolution because their emotions take over the conversation and override their logic. Scheduling a meeting gives you an opportunity to prepare your heart and your thoughts for navigating the discussion.

Before the meeting, describe the issue in writing as you are aware of it. Keep in mind that the "presenting" issue is not always the real issue, but you have to start somewhere. If you can clearly state your thoughts about the disagreement without reacting to one another, you will have a much better chance of resolving the situation.

At the meeting, proceed along the following steps to SOLVE the issue:

- *Seek God together.* Pray together and ask God to give you wisdom to work through the issue.

- *Open the conversation.* Decide who is going to share first. There are a number of ways you can manage this. For instance, you can buy a small piece of carpet that you pass back and forth. Whoever has the floor will do the talking. The one who does not have the floor will do nothing but listen. When you are done, pass the floor to your spouse and take your turn listening. You can also choose a small ball that you roll back and forth with the statement, "The ball is in your court." You can even use a piece of paper that you take turns holding so you can "get on the same page." These are simple tools to help you stay on track while you keep your emotions in check. Keep the dialogue going until you feel the environment soften between the two of you.

- *Look deeper.* After both of you have shared sufficiently, ask, "What do you think the real issue is?" It may be the issue you've been talking about or it may be something else. It could be a reaction to something from your past or something you are afraid of. It is also possible that stress has risen in your life and you are taking the stress out on each other. It is also possible that you are upset with your spouse about the best traits in his or her life. Your spouse may have made a decision without your consent or made social commitments that take you beyond your comfort level.

- *Verify options.* Once you've identified the real issue, discuss possible solutions. We have found it best to write down the ideas we come up with rather than trust them to memory. If one of the ideas becomes an obvious solution and you can both agree on it, commit to it and begin to implement your agreement. If the solution is not obvious, pray together and then set another meeting to discuss the solution. This will give you a day or two to consider the ideas you came up with. Since emotions rise and fall in their intensity, time will help you think through your solutions when your emotional intensity diminishes.

- *Evolve into the answer.* Get back together in a day or two to discuss a solution. Be patient at this point. Some challenges don't actually have solutions. You may have a special needs child who regularly creates stress in your relationship. You may have had a financial setback that will take years to recover from. You may have faced a health issue that has forced your lifestyle to change. You adjust to these stresses, but you don't actually fix them. You look for ways to grow together while you live an unconventional lifestyle, but you don't ever really return to a normal life. As you navigate it together, you will discover a depth in your love that is your reward for taking the journey together.

The Spontaneous Approach

This approach takes the most self-control and relational skill to get right. In this approach, you deal with issues as they come up. You don't wait, you don't reschedule, and you don't give yourself time to gather your composure. You just jump in and try to get to the heart of the matter. A few skills will help you in this approach:

- *Insulate.* Use "I" statements instead of "you" statements. This is easy to write about and it is easy to say you will do this when you are calm, but it is a very different matter when you are upset with each other. "You" statements sound like accusations when they are mixed with negative emotions. "You did this," "You are so inconsiderate," "You were being selfish," may be statements of truth, but they easily illicit defensive responses. Your ability to use "I" statements will determine your ability to successfully work through these discussions. "I was surprised by what happened," "I am very upset by this situation," "I was shocked when this happened and I reacted very strongly," are statements that do not avoid the subject but give your spouse an opportunity to respond without getting defensive.

- *Investigate.* Take time to relieve the pressure by describing what you believe the issue is. The purpose of this phase is to lower the intensity of the emotional climate between the two of you. Ask, "What is the real issue we are facing?" Just like all conflicts, the goal is to identify the issues that are at the heart of your reaction so you can find a positive direction to move.

- *Identify.* Brainstorm solutions. Verbally investigate possible ways to address the conflict. Take enough time to explore possibilities to see if a new solution surfaces that wasn't clear in the heat of the moment.

- *Initiate.* Commit to a course of action based on your conclusions.

- *Interconnect.* Before you end your discussion, seek to discover what it is you love about each other that caused this disagreement. The reason you have such intense discussions with each other is the emotional connection you share. You are highly attractive to your spouse, and when the dark side of these attractive traits show themselves, they create intense negative responses. Since these negative responses are attached to the things you love about your mate, they can easily be turned positive. This is why "make-up" sex is a common experience for married couples. They are upset with each other, argue through the issue, reach a conclusion, then suddenly rediscover their attraction to one another. This is where you want all of your arguments to end so that disagreements work for you rather than tear you apart.

The Delayed Approach

If scheduling a meeting or having a spontaneous discussion doesn't work for you, try taking a break for a short time before you work your way through the issue. The purpose of the break is to calm down your emotions and get yourself back to a more rational place.

It is more reliable if you choose a specific time to get back together, but you may be able to say, "As soon as we calm down, let's get back together." If you take this approach, you will want to check in with each other every couple of hours to see if you have calmed down. If you do not diligently check in, it's likely you will ignore the issue and conclude that time has taken care of everything. This is like planting a landmine in the middle of your home. If you do this enough times, those mines will eventually erupt and cause severe damage to the relationship. It is much better to deal with the issues as individual discussions rather than waiting for a compound problem to unleash itself.

When you get together, you will want to follow the same steps as above:

- *Insulate.* Use "I" statements instead of "you" statements.
- *Investigate.* Take time to relieve the pressure by describing what you believe the issue is. Ask, "What is the real issue we are facing?"
- *Identify.* Brainstorm solutions.
- *Initiate.* Commit to a course of action based on your conclusions.
- *Interconnect.* Before you end your discussion, seek to discover what it is you love about each other that caused this disagreement.

A Honda and Hurt Feelings

I (Pam) drive a Honda CRV. It's a cute little SUV that hauls books around well and doesn't go too fast, which is good for me. The spare tire is mounted on the back, and Bill bought me a tire cover from the University of Louisville, since our middle son attends school there. It makes my car easy to pick out in a parking lot, and it keeps me emotionally connected with my son who lives 2000 miles away. Every time I see the Cardinal mascot on the back of my car, I pray for Zach. Well, Bill was driving my CRV on the freeway, and the tire cover blew off.

"I don't know if you noticed, but the tire cover blew off your car," he told me later.

"Oh, no!" I said. "We have to get it replaced. Zach's feelings are going to be hurt."

"No they won't. To him it's just a tire cover."

"They will too. Zach is a very sensitive young man, and this is important to him. We have to replace this right away. In fact, you're going to be in Louisville next week so you can take care of it."

"We'll see. If it works out, I'll get a new one, but I'm not going out of my way to look for one while I'm there."

"So, you don't really care about Zach's feelings?"

"I care about Zach's feelings. I just don't think this is about his emotions."

"Oh, you think I'm overreacting?"

"No, I just think we approach things like this differently. You're really good at being emotionally invested in Zach and the tire cover, but I just can't go there. Don't let me stop you, but please don't expect me to react the same way. I love your emotional vibrancy as long as I get to watch."

"You are such a man. I love you all the way from here to Louisville, but you are such a man. Will you pleeeeaaaase try to get a new tire cover when you're with Zach. I think *you* will like the way I react when I see it on my car!"

Bill got the tire cover—and I was right, he did love my reaction!

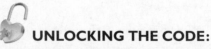

UNLOCKING THE CODE:
Dinner and Dialogue for a Heart-to-Heart Connection

Each of you identify which problem solving method you feel most comfortable with. Then share if you think another approach might better help your relationship move forward. Thank your spouse for hanging in there with you in how you approach life.

If you are brave, tackle an issue in your relationship that you need a solution to and use one of the methods above to seek a solution. Pick an easy issue for the first run—maybe the solution to world peace, the national deficit, or how to raise the Dow can be put off for another day.

■ ■ ■

After a quarrel, a wife said to her husband, "You know, I was a fool when I married you."

The husband replied, "Yes, dear, but I was in love and didn't notice."

ABOVE THE LINE
_____

BELOW THE LINE

(RING)

"Hello?"

"Hi, honey, this is Daddy. Is Mommy near the phone?"

"No, Daddy. She's upstairs in the bedroom with Uncle Paul."

After a brief pause, Daddy says, "But honey, you haven't got an Uncle Paul."

"Oh yes I do, and he's upstairs with Mommy right now."

"Uh, okay then…this is what I want you to do. Put the phone down on the table, run upstairs and knock on the bedroom door, and shout to Mommy that Daddy's car just pulled into the driveway."

"Okay, Daddy, just a minute" A few minutes later the little girl came back to the phone. "I did it, Daddy."

"And what happened, honey?"

"Well, Mommy got all scared, jumped up, and ran down the stairs screaming. Then she tripped over the rug, hit her head, and now she isn't moving at all!"

"Oh no! What about your Uncle Paul?"

"He jumped out the back window and into the swimming pool. But I guess he didn't know that you took out the water last week to clean it. He hit the bottom of the pool, and I think he's dead!"

(*Long pause*)

"Swimming pool? Is this 486-5731?"

Chapter 6

Intimacy

"The fruit of the Spirit is...faithfulness..."

Steve and Tricia desperately needed some time together. Their life was in high gear with busy careers, two active children, and vigorous commitments in their community. They loved each other deeply, but were so busy with life their intimacy was fading. Steve knew he had to take action.

Steve called his sister to ask if she would watch the kids so he could spend some time with Tricia alone. His sister was not married and loved spending time with her niece and nephew, so she agreed. The date was set for a Sunday afternoon, but Steve's sister had a commitment at six that night so she could watch the kids only until five.

Steve and Tricia went to church together, and then enjoyed a leisurely lunch. As they were talking, Steve noticed that his wife was struggling to reconnect with him. He knew that they would need to spend the afternoon talking if they were going to rediscover the intimacy in their relationship. He knew of a lake nearby where he knew Tricia liked to go, so they stopped by the store, bought a loaf of bread, and headed for the lakeside.

As they walked toward the waterfront, ducks began to congregate. They both took a little bread and began feeding the ducks. They talked and fed the ducks. They walked and fed the ducks. They sat and fed the ducks. They got caught up in the experience and lost track of time. Steve was thoroughly enjoying the afternoon because Tricia was laughing and flirting. Tricia thoroughly enjoyed the afternoon because she felt valuable to Steve once again. Almost accidently, Steve glanced at his watch and noticed that it was five o'clock.

"We have to go, Tricia! My sister has to be somewhere at six, and we told her we'd be home at five."

They scurried home to relieve a much appreciated sister. Tricia went straight to the kids while Steve took time to thank his sister.

"So, how did it go?" she asked with a look of curiosity.

"It was great. Thank you so much. We spent a lot of time feeding the ducks."

The curious look changed to a sly smile as she said, "Feeding the ducks, huh?" She winked at Steve and gently touched his arm, then grabbed her things and headed out the door.

Steve found Tricia and told her, "My sister thinks we made love when we were out, and she thinks we call it *feeding the ducks*."

They shared a good laugh together and agreed it was the perfect ending to a very good day. They decided it would only be right if they ended the day "feeding the ducks."

How to Know for Sure

How do you let your spouse know that you are interested in sexual interaction? For centuries, husband and wives have been in love and have longed to share that love in a romantic, sexual relationship. It has been an interesting dance, to say the least, and we all have a difficult time communicating that now is a good time.

Pam and I were sharing at a seminar our word picture that men are like waffles and women are like spaghetti.

Pam said to the crowd, "Men like to go to their favorite, easy boxes to rest and recharge. But God kind of helped us ladies out because men's favorite boxes are actually shaped like boxes. The TV is shaped like a box. The computer screen is shaped like a box. The refrigerator is shaped like a box. The football field is shaped like a box. The baseball diamond is shaped like a box. The basketball court is shaped like a box. And the bed is shaped like a box. In fact, that sex box is a man's favorite box to go to when he is stressed. It's like that free square in the middle of a bingo card, and he can get to that box from every other box on his waffle."

The crowd erupted in laughter as they realized the truth of what Pam had just said. For the rest of the conference, every time we mentioned the word sex, the crowd would respond, "Bingo!" During the afternoon break, one of the couples found a plaque with the words, *Born to Bingo.* That plaque hangs in our office as a joyful reminder. Recently we were guest speakers on a cruise line, and the recreational staff wore shirts that read, "Have You Been Bingoed Today?" We had to have them! The question, "Do you want to play some bingo?" has taken on a whole new meaning in our home.

> We all have codes or ways to say, "Baby, I want *you!*"

Fire on the Couch!

We did a conference in the south, and they were a little shy when it came to talking out loud about sex. They had an icebreaker game akin to *The Newlywed Game.* Husbands and wives answered questions, and the couple that matched the most answers won a prize. One of the questions was, "What would your spouse say is their favorite date?"

All the women said something like, "Go to dinner then go home early."

When the husbands came back, one of the men answered, "Go to dinner, maybe a movie, but go home early and light a fire in the fireplace and a fire on the couch!"

So we learned that in the south, they don't "have sex." They "go home early" then "light a fire on the couch!"

We all have codes or ways to say, "Baby, I want *you!*" Or just the opposite—when we are not in the mood, we can give off clues that are pretty easy to read.

What's the Combination?

The idea of needing some kind of code to let your spouse know that you are interested sexually has been around as long as love itself. Seems like often, men and women just can't get on the same wave length on when, where, or how often to enjoy "red-hot monogamy."

> A man wakes up his wife during the night with a glass of water in one hand and two aspirins in the other. She asks, "What's this for?"
>
> "This is for your headache," he says.
>
> "But I don't have a headache."
>
> He smiles and says, "Gotcha!"

Men and women just don't hear the same messages in the area of sexuality:

> The wife says: "This place is a mess! C'mon, you and I need to clean up. Your stuff is lying on the floor, and if we don't do laundry right now, you'll have no clothes to wear."
>
> What the husband hears: Blah, blah, blah, blah, C'MON blah, blah, blah, YOU AND I blah, blah, ON THE FLOOR blah, blah, blah, RIGHT NOW blah, blah, blah, blah, blah, NO CLOTHES.

Breaking the Code to Connect

Sexual love is one of the most fascinating and intricate activities that humans engage in. It is a great workout, but it is more than just physical exercise. It is a great way to connect with the one you love, but it is more than just communication. It will result in offspring who will reflect in their lives all that is important to you, but it is more than just procreation. Sex is the knitting together of two individuals physically, emotionally, spiritually, and adventurously.

A satisfying sexual relationship involves every part of your being. You can't just say, "So, do you want to have sex tonight?" and expect things to go well. If you approach sex too casually, you may engage the physical side, but you leave out the emotional and spiritual. If you make it all about connecting your hearts, you will engage the emotional and spiritual side but miss out on the physical and adventurous side. More than any other activity on earth, sex is an "all of the above" experience.

The most valuable possessions are put in a safe. If you know the combination to the safe, you can access these valuables any time you want. If you do not know the combination, you are locked out and can only imagine what might be behind the locked door. If your possessions are sort of valuable, you will put them behind a rather simple lock. If they are highly valuable, you will invest in a more rugged and more complicated locking system.

> From God's point of view, sexual love is highly valuable.

The High Value of Your Love

From God's point of view, sexual love is highly valuable. It is valuable for three reasons. First, *it is intensely personal.* When you engage in a sexual activity, you make yourself completely vulnerable. You expose your bodies to one another, and you expose your souls to one another. It is impossible to have interacted sexually without igniting your mind, your body, and your emotions.

For instance, during sexual intercourse, the hormone oxytocin is released in the woman's body that causes her to "feel in love" with her partner.[13] As a result, the relationship intensifies. She will dream about the experience, evaluate the experience, and relive the emotions of the experience many times. If the emotional climate of the relationship matches her newfound feelings of love, she will settle in and commit herself at a deeper level. If the emotional climate does not match, she will react negatively and create turmoil in their interaction.

Second, it is valuable because *it promotes trust.* You get naked only with someone you trust. You release sexual energy only with someone you trust. You give satisfying sexual experiences only to someone you trust. Trust is, in fact, the key to a woman's ability to experience orgasm.

Trust is also the key to a long-term enjoyable sex life. After a while, you will have tried pretty much everything you want to try sexually with each other. What keeps the fire burning after the experimentation has been exhausted is your willingness to talk about your sexual love as you go through the various seasons of life together. Sex is different at 35 than it was at 25, at 40 than it was at 30, and at 60 than it was at 40. Discussing your intimate life as your body and your life changes keeps it truly intimate throughout your life.

Trust is, coincidentally, the key to having a successful relationship with Jesus, for "without faith it is impossible to please God" (Hebrews 11:6) and those who fear the Lord trust in the Lord (Psalm 115:11). Unlocking the potential in your sexual love for each other expands your ability to trust, which will increase your ability to follow God's leading in your life. And vice versa, a deep trust for God will give you the ability to trust your mate, which will translate into passion in the bedroom.

Third, sex is valuable because *it is mysterious*. It is a physical experience, but it is much more. It involves the exchange of fluids between your bodies, but it is not just a biological process. It stirs intense emotions in you, but it is more than an emotional experience.

Then you have the mystery of why God made us so different in this area. I (Bill) am still amazed at our differences after three decades of being in love. It intrigues me that I can be ready for sex so quickly while it takes showing Pam interest for a while before she is ready. It fascinates me that she can be so interested after the warm up period, to the point that it is hard to keep up at times. Then I am amused that I fall asleep so quickly afterwards while she is energized for at least a couple of hours. I know God did this so that there would be greater variety in our expressions of love, but there will always be a mysterious side to sex.

> God has wired each man to be instantly attracted to his wife through a long list of simple stimuli.

Impulses and Interactions

For a detailed discussion of the differences between men and women when it comes to sex, see our book, *Red-Hot Monogamy*, but for now let's just say that men get ready for sex by *impulse* while women get ready for sex by *interaction*.

Any of the following activities will stimulate a man's *impulse* and have him ready to love his wife:

- She walks by
- She gets in the shower
- She gets out of the shower
- She winks at him
- She looks at him with a loving expression
- She gets undressed
- She gets dressed
- She bends forward so he gets a peak at her breasts
- She leans forward and looks back at him
- She whispers any sexual suggestion
- She suggests they go out on a date
- She suggests they stay home

You get the idea. God has wired each man to be instantly attracted to his wife through a long list of simple stimuli.

Any of the following activities will tap into a wife's desire to *interact* and begin the process of preparing her to sexually interact with her husband:

- Listening to her with interest
- Treating her opinions as if they are important
- Helping with housework
- Doing a favor

- Hugging just because you are happy to see her (especially if it is just a little longer than your normal hugs)
- Spending time together having fun
- Finishing a project that is important to her
- Lowering her stress level
- Getting her to laugh
- Giving her time off from the kids to relax
- Giving an unhurried massage
- Caressing her body in patient foreplay
- Playing with the kids and enjoying it
- Planning a vacation together
- Complimenting her for no particular reason
- Saying, "I'm sorry," when you have made a mistake
- Saying no to something else so you can spend time with her
- Bragging about her in front of friends

The list could go on because your wife loves to know that she is important to you, and when she sees that message in action, she gets attracted to you.

Since sexual love is so valuable, God has hidden it behind a combination. Couples who apply the combination regularly discover that sex is a great enhancement to their lives. They laugh about it, look forward to it, and blush when they consider what other people would think if they knew how good it is. Couples who try to force the safe open discover that sex can be a real up and down experience. They put up with each other, ignore each other, and misunderstand each other. They hope that other people never find out how it really is between them.

The combination for a successful sex life is reported in Ephesians 5:33, "each one of you also must love his wife as he loves himself, and the wife must respect her husband." The combination that unlocks a woman's interest is love, while the combination that unlocks a man's interest is respect. We see the combination in action in the Song of Solomon as Solomon and Shulammite unlock the potential in their love for each other.

Decoder Moment:

Impulse: Guys, look at the impulse list and see which action revs your engine the quickest and share that with your wife.

Interaction: Gals, look at the list of interactions and share with your husband your favorite interaction with him that sets your mood.

The Love Combination

Your wife has been designed in such a way that she will respond when you reach her heart. In other words: *If you love her heart, she will give you her body.*

Solomon modeled for us husbands how to love our wives in a way that causes them to be sexually interested in us.

Be affirming to her. Move past just saying nice things and make her feel important with your words. Women have a habit of continually evaluating themselves. She looks at herself in the mirror and concludes, "I'm not pretty enough, smart enough, capable enough, sexy enough, old enough, young enough," and so on. She doesn't mean to be so self-conscious, but she cannot find the off switch that makes it stop. She may have a good day today, but the thoughts of inadequacy can rise to the surface tomorrow with very little stimulus. A thought, a look, or a setback can resurrect her insecurities and get them swirling.

> Since sexual love is so valuable, God has hidden it behind a combination. The combination that unlocks a woman's interest is love, while the combination that unlocks a man's interest is respect.

You can help her by reaffirming her importance to you every chance you get. Since men are problem solvers, we want to boil this scenario in our wives down to a formula. We want to resolve in her life once and for all so she never has to bring it up again. That is the equivalent to her saying to you, "Honey, I want us to have one really great night of sex that will take care of your sexual need once and for all!"

In the Song of Solomon 1:6, Shulammite is feeling this insecurity and says to her husband,

> Do not stare at me because I am dark,
>   because I am darkened by the sun.
> My mother's sons were angry with me
>   and made me take care of the vineyards;
>   my own vineyard I have neglected.

She grew up in an agricultural family and was made to work outdoors. As a result, her skin was tanned in a society that treasured light skin that had been pampered. She is concerned that her husband will find her unattractive compared to the other women he interacts with in his professional life. He responds with affirming words,

> How beautiful you are, my darling!
>   Oh, how beautiful!
>   (Song of Solomon 1:15)

You can almost see his knees weaken as he thinks about the beauty of his wife. He never grew tired of her need to know she was beautiful and highly valuable to him. As a result, they had an outstanding love life.

> Move past just saying nice things and make her feel important with your words.

Be fascinated with her. Move past just noticing her and stay curious about how she really works. Your wife needs time to respond sexually. She slowly warms up to your love. Sex is an all-consuming event in her life that requires her to yield to the experience in order to truly enjoy it. She never has and never will be ready as quickly as you. As a result, foreplay is as much a part of your love life as intercourse. For her, it is all connected.

Once when we were really busy, Bill ran home to pick up the

briefcase he had forgotten. He zipped past me and grabbed my waist and said, "I wish I was independently wealthy and could just stay home and love you all day long!" He gave me a kiss and darted out the door. It was three days later before we had a day off together. Usually when we have been living a hectic pace, it takes us a little while to feel emotionally connected enough to be ready for sexual connection. It often takes the whole day to warm up to each other. But that morning I woke up amorous! Bill said, "Pam, don't get me wrong, I love this. But usually when we have been living such a fast pace then get a day together it takes you a while to warm up, but today..."

> Foreplay is as much a part of your love life as intercourse.

"Well, Bill, four days ago you told me you wished you were independently wealthy and could just stay home and love me all day long. Four days ago you started foreplay, so when your body showed up today, I was ready!"

How Intriguing!

Your wife will greatly appreciate if you approach her with fascination. Since her body responds very differently from yours, you can approach her with either impatience or intrigue. She has a much greater capacity for sexual response than you do. During any sexual experience with you, she can have a single orgasm or multiple orgasms (or dare we say, no orgasm?). She can enjoy sexual stimulation for minutes or hours. She can maintain sexual interest for the entire evening.

> If you want to have a great sex life with your wife, make it your ambition to be a great friend to her.

This can be humbling for you as a man since you turn on and off pretty quickly, and you can never experience the height and length of sexual stimulation that she can. You will never understand experientially what it is like for her, but you can remain curious throughout your life. Your willingness to explore and experiment with ways she is comfortable with will help both of you discover a whole new world together.

In the Song of Solomon 2:16, Shulammite says to her lover,

> My lover is mine and I am his;
>> he browses among the lilies.

This couple's sex code revolved around gardening terms. She grew up on a farm and apparently loved nature, so they used farming terms to refer to their love life. When she says he "browses among the lilies," she is complimenting him for taking his time and exploring the potential of her body. She obviously enjoyed his patient exploration, because she encourages him in the very next verse to continue all night long!

Be interactive with her. Make moves to be involved in her life. Every activity of your life together is part of her sexual interest in you. When you spend time listening to her, her interest grows. When you walk with her and pray for your family, her interest grows. When you play with the kids, you look sexier to her. We had a wife tell us just this week, "I wish he would understand that it turns me on when he helps around the house." In fact, women have shared these things as turn-ons:

- When he gets on the floor and plays Barbie with our six-year-old daughter
- When he is covered with paint from repainting our bathroom all day
- When he is standing over the stove and I am sitting with a drink watching him cook
- When he has a vacuum in his hands

Your wife longs to know that she matters to you. It is the switch that turns on her sex drive. You can fight it or you can accept it, but you will never change it. A woman who believes her husband wants to be her best friend will find him an interesting lover.

In the Song of Solomon 7:10-13, Shulammite invites Solomon to go to the countryside to enjoy the blossoming of the flowers and the growth of the vineyards. They, in essence, are taking a day of sightseeing. They will travel together, walk together, talk together, and discover together. In her heart, this means they are knitting their lives together. She recognized the power this simple activity would have on her heart, so she makes reference to what she has stored up for

Every activity of your life together is part of her sexual interest in you.

her lover. If you want to have a great sex life with your wife, make it your ambition to be a great friend to her.

The Respect Combination

Your husband, on the other hand, has been designed in such a way that he will respond to your beauty and your sexual confidence. Don't think, however, that you have to be the most beautiful woman around or that you have to be an animal in bed (although it's okay if you want to be). All you have to do is accept that your husband married you because he found you attractive and be willing to mature in your love life. Your husband is physically wired for consistent sexual activity. He is constantly aware of the demands his body places on him. He loves his sex drive and is frustrated by it all at the same. As a result: *If you love his body, he will give you his heart.*

Shulammite modeled for us wives how to love our husbands in a way that causes them to want to be with us.

Be adventurous with him. Move beyond being willing to have sex and explore your preferences together. Men love the active side of sex. It isn't that they don't like the emotional and spiritual connection because, at times, they long to be connected to their wives in a reassuring way. It's just that testosterone runs in every cell of his body encouraging him to take an aggressive, visceral approach to life.

Your husband is physically wired for consistent sexual activity.

Most of us men know that we need to keep our desires in check because the aggressiveness can take over our lives. At the same time, we secretly hope that our wives will develop an appetite for sexual activity that will make it fun and adventurous. We are not proponents for sexual activity that is dangerous in any way,

Most of us men secretly hope that our wives will develop an appetite for sexual activity that will make it fun and adventurous.

but we also believe that God has gifted people with creativity and a high capacity for sexual intimacy. It is healthy, therefore, for married couples to explore the possibilities in their sexual love and to make decisions together about what they will and will not try.

The Song of Solomon actually begins with Shulammite asking Solomon to make love to her.

> Let him kiss me with the kisses of his mouth—
>> for your love is more delightful than wine.
> Pleasing is the fragrance of your perfumes;
>> your name is like perfume poured out.
>> No wonder the maidens love you!
> Take me away with you—let us hurry!
>> Let the king bring me into his chambers.
>> (Song of Solomon 1:2-4)

She continues to fan her adventurous side,

> How handsome you are, my lover!
>> Oh, how charming!
> And our bed is verdant.
>> (1:16)

A verdant bed is perhaps a reference to the beds found in vineyards and desert oases where people could rest. She is referencing having sex out of doors—that is way beyond making love with the lights on!

She continues the invitation to adventure when she says,

> Let us go early to the vineyards
>> to see if the vines have budded,
> if their blossoms have opened,
>> and if the pomegranates are in bloom—
>> there I will give you my love.

The mandrakes send out their fragrance,
    and at our door is every delicacy,
both new and old,
    that I have stored up for you, my lover.
     (7:12-13)

She is inviting him to experience intimacy that is both "old"—things they are both comfortable with—and "new"—things she is willing to try.

In *The 10 Best Decisions a Couple Can Make*, we review what God okays in the bedroom. God gives much freedom behind closed doors. You can say *yes* to an intimate activity if you:

Yield to one another—Everything done is agreed upon; no one should feel forced.

> Each of you should look not only to your own interests, but also to the interests of others. Your attitude should be the same as that of Christ Jesus...taking the very nature of a servant (Philippians 2:4-5).

Extend it in love—Nothing that would risk your health, life, or reputation. (Jail is kind of a mood killer!)

> And over all these virtues put on love, which binds them all together in perfect unity (Colossians 3:14).

Secure it with privacy—Should only be you two.

> Marriage should be honored by all, and the marriage bed kept pure, for God will judge the adulterer and all the sexually immoral (Hebrews 13:4).

Get a good lock and a good attitude, and you will likely create a good time for you both.

Be interested in him. Your husband's body is much different than your own. He is strong, and every cell in his body is designed to react to the stimuli of life. He sees challenges and wants to conquer them. He doesn't mean to treat you as a challenge to overcome, but he is nagged by his body. Every few days, semen builds up and silently screams at him for release.

He has an ongoing argument with himself. *Wow! She is really beautiful. I wonder if she longs for me as much as I long for her right now. Bill, it's time for dinner and the whole family is waiting. I know but it wouldn't take long, and I would be better company at the table. I know, it's not time, but I hope tonight is the night. Come to think of it, I hope tomorrow is the night also. Calm down, Bill. You need to pay bills tonight, and you promised to help your son with his homework. Why can't he do his homework himself? I sure wish Pam could have finished that with him earlier so we could go to bed early. I wonder how fast we can get it done. No, no! Just help him. He's your son.*

We know you can't give in every time we want to hook up with you, but we sure love it when you are sensitive to the fact that our sex drive is always asking for attention.

This is the strangest part of a man's life. No other subject and no other activity consumes his thinking like sex. Most men I (Bill) know wish they could turn it off. We are frustrated that there is no off switch we can throw that will calm down the aching in our groin. It is inconvenient, unreasonable, demanding, and childish. We can describe it to you in detail, but we haven't figured out how to calm it down. We can discipline it so that it doesn't run our lives, but we cannot make it go away. Every few days the urge will be back, and it will nag at us until it is released. This is why the question, "How often can we have sex?" is such a big one for men.

We don't want you to have to carry the burden for this struggle, so we try to not put pressure on you, but it is still there. A wife who says to herself, *this is the man I love, and God created him with a sex drive. It is more aggressive than anything I truly understand, but I will remain curious about what it is like for him. I will do my best to make this our challenge rather than just his.*

In the Song of Solomon 5:2, we see Solomon in one of these mildly desperate moments. He is longing for his wife, and his sexual desire is strong when he knocks on her door and pleads,

> "Open to me, my sister, my darling,
>   my dove, my flawless one.
> My head is drenched with dew,
>   my hair with the dampness of the night."

He is rattling off compliments, giving silly reasons why she should succumb and begging her to be interested. We know you can't give in every time we want to hook up with you, but we sure love it when you are sensitive to the fact that our sex drive is always asking for attention.

Shulammite accepted that at times sexual activity ought to have a desperate tone to it. In Song of Solomon 3, she went to the streets to look for her husband because she could not wait any longer.

> Scarcely had I passed them
>   when I found the one my heart loves.
> I held him and would not let him go
>   till I had brought him to my mother's house,
>   to the room of the one who conceived me.
>   (v. 4)

In chapter 2 she states her desperation a little creatively,

> Strengthen me with raisins,
>   refresh me with apples,
>   for I am faint with love.
>   (v. 5)

She longs for intimate time with her husband as we hunger for food. Guys can definitely relate to that word picture!

As husbands, we don't expect you to be this crazy for us all the time, but we sure love it when you pursue us with a little bit of desperation.

Be proud of him. Men are success-oriented creatures. By this we mean that they long to do what they know they are good at. They spend a lot of time at work when they discover they are good at it. They spend time with musical instruments when they discover they have talent. They will romance their wives if they discover they are good at it. Conversely, they avoid whatever they conclude they are bad at.

> It is a deliberate choice to stay focused on his strengths and find ways to say, "I am proud of you."

As a result, a man is drawn to people who are proud of him. Since you are his wife, you are aware of his deficiencies, annoying habits, and shortcomings. It is a challenge to build him up in his strength without commenting on his weaknesses. Once you open up to it, it is easy to give his shortcomings more attention than his strengths because they are irritating. It is a deliberate choice on your part to stay focused on his strengths and find ways to say, "I am proud of you."

In Song of Solomon 3:9-11, Shulammite publicly compliments Solomon for his building projects, the skill with which he built his throne, and his leadership ability. She could just as easily have said that he had overdone it and spent too much money. Instead, she built him up, pointed out his strengths, and trusted God to work on his weaknesses.

She also complimented him behind closed doors. She continues her praises in chapter 5:

> My lover is radiant and ruddy,
>   outstanding among ten thousand.
>   (v. 10)

She then goes on to praise him head to toe. Twice in Song of Songs she says,

> His left arm is under my head,
>   and his right arm embraces me.
>   (2:6, 8:3)

This is her verbalizing, in the midst of his lovemaking, what he does that she loves. This is the ultimate compliment to a man. Build him up in the bedroom, and he will rule in the board room.

There are few things, other than nakedness, that turn on a man like sincere compliments. This is really what flirting is all about. When you use your body language, tone of voice, and words to say, "You are a hunk. I am so glad I am with you, and I feel sorry for all the other women who don't get to enjoy your love," you are irresistible!

Midlife Madness

In midlife, the roles can switch. She might want sex more often than he does. He might feel a need to perform, and if his penis won't cooperate, he battles a sense of failure. Who wants to feel that way? The popularity of drugs such as Viagra and Levitra shows the number of men who deal with this issue. (And if men are dealing with this issue, so are their wives). The danger in this scenario is for a wife to long for her husband but not know how to meet his needs. Couples in this stage of life need higher sexual and communication skills because more and more topics and issues will need to be discussed as a couple ages together.

Our society is filled with evidence that romance and sexual expression are pervasive needs in people's lives. Middle-aged women are having affairs and leaving their families because they found someone who seems to patiently understand their emotional needs. These may be face-to-face encounters or they may be online relationships, but they are having a powerful influence over many women. Men are aggressively drifting into risky behavior, such as affairs, pornography, and online lovers in an attempt to find someone who accepts their sexuality. In these cases, people are settling for a sexual counterfeit instead of the real thing.

In our book *Red-Hot Monogamy*, we train couples to make their sex life a high priority. The book outlines an eight-week plan for connecting sexually and includes "hands on homework" (pun completely intended). It is homework you want to do! There are over 200 red-hot ideas to try. The key is to become sexual partners that care enough to please each other by lowering the fear walls that prevent you from expressing your love to one another.

The Freedom of Faithfulness

The answer to sexual satisfaction through all the seasons of life is faithfulness. It is the glue that connects trust to our relationships because it removes the other options. When you commit to be faithful to your spouse, you have to work it out together because no one else can even enter the discussion.

Too many of us have a passive view of faithfulness. We think to ourselves, *I am faithful. I guess I just need to hang in here and hope it turns out well. I hope my spouse becomes a good lover, but if not, I'll just have to be bored for the rest of my life.*

> The answer to sexual satisfaction through all the seasons of life is faithfulness.

That is not faithfulness, it is resignation. Faithfulness says, *I am going to put my best into this relationship. I hope my spouse will do the same, but I will be the best partner, best lover, best provider, and best friend to my spouse that I can possibly be. I will remain curious about his or her needs, and I will commit to personal growth that will make me a better partner every year. I don't think my spouse will be able to resist if I become a better sexual partner year after year.*

This is the intent of 1 Corinthians 7:4-6.

> The wife does not have authority over her own body, but the husband does; and likewise also the husband does not have authority over his own body, but the wife does. Stop depriving one another, except by agreement for a time, so that you may devote yourselves to prayer, and come together again so that Satan will not tempt you because of your lack of self-control. But this I say by way of concession, not of command.

Each of us has a "marital duty" to fulfill one another sexually. This means we should become students of each other's sexual needs to the point that we can meet them on a regular basis. Each of us has the privilege of the other's body. When a man and woman marry, they are saying to each other, "My body no longer belongs to me alone. It is yours also. I am giving my body to you so that you can experience a satisfying sexual life."

Shulammite explains it this way,

> I belong to my lover,
>> and his desire is for me.
>>> (Song of Solomon 7:10)

Finally, our sexual interaction helps us avoid temptation. Satan works overtime in the arena of sexual temptation. He has been doing it for centuries, and he has sophisticated schemes to distract us. If, however, your spouse is satisfied at home and you are consistently growing in your ability to express love to each other, it is unlikely that any temptation will be attractive enough to take you away from a good thing.

"My body no longer belongs to me alone. It is yours also."

Solomon's wife puts the priority of faithfulness in a beautiful way:

> Place me like a seal over your heart,
>> like a seal on your arm;
> for love is as strong as death,
>> its jealousy unyielding as the grave.
> It burns like blazing fire,
>> like a mighty flame.
> Many waters cannot quench love;
>> rivers cannot wash it away.
> If one were to give
>> all the wealth of his house for love,
>> it would be utterly scorned.
>>> (Song of Solomon 8:6-7)

If you want a love stronger than death, so ablaze with passion that many waters cannot quench it, then place your mate as a seal over your heart. Stand at the foot of your bed, place your hand over the heart of your spouse, and pray for one another, "God, I place my wife/husband as a seal over my heart. Please send your love into our hearts and our home. Amen."

EVIDENCE COLLECTION:

Foster Faithfulness

Each of you circle the faithfulness decisions you have already made:

- I will not have sex with anyone other than my spouse.
- I will not "date" another person by having a meal alone or meeting alone with a person of the opposite sex.
- I will protect my sex life by avoiding sexual counterfeits such as pornography and explicit movies or TV.
- I will not reconnect to old flames through e-mail, texting, online chatrooms, etc.
- I will pursue my mate by doing something nice for him or her every day.
- I will romance my spouse by saying words to build up him or her.
- I will caress my spouse by choosing significant encouraging touch without the pressure of performing sex for me.
- I will tell my spouse when I desire him or her.
- I will invest time, energy, and money to romance my spouse.
- I will look for ways to fulfill my mate's sexual desires and needs.
- I will be a best friend to my spouse.
- I will seek to lower the stress on my spouse.
- I will seek to be a support to my mate to help him or her achieve their God-given potential.

Set a date to talk with your spouse about what he or she has done that helps you trust them. Compliment each other for the things you have decided to do already. If there is one thing on the list that wasn't marked and it would help you feel freer behind the bedroom door, share what it is and why it would help you.

UNLOCKING THE CODE:
Dinner and Dialogue for a Heart-to-Heart Connection

Getting in Sync

There are a number of possible ways you can create faithfulness that will boost your sexual love for one another:

1. Identify a code word that says, "I am definitely in the mood to be with you." To help you identify code words that exist in your relationship, consider these real-life examples from other couples:

   - Peter and Joan love movies and have both worked in the entertainment industry at various times. They once overheard some people ask, "Have you ever watched a show with a young lady?" They thought it was cute that sex was referred to as "watching a show together," so they adopted it for their relationship.

   - Sandy is shy and has a difficult time saying the word *sex*, let alone saying to Robert that she would love to engage in sex with him. At the same time, she loves him very much and enjoys their sexual interaction. She decided to let him know about her mood by writing a number on the bathroom mirror with lipstick. A "10" on the mirror means you probably ought to come home at lunch while a "1" means you might as well play golf after work.

   - We used to ask, "Would you like to take a nap?" Since

we are over forty now, "Would you like to take a nap?" means "Would you like to take a nap?" So "Bingo" has been a great addition to our vocabulary instead.

- Ricky noticed that Briana often wore a red shirt when she was interested in him sexually. He bought her a red tank top on Valentine's Day that year. For his birthday, Briana decided to return the favor. Red-shirt days are usually good days in their house!

2. Wives—choose one of the elements of the Respect Combination to practice this week. You can do something adventurous with your husband that you have been embarrassed to try. You can show special interest in him and ask him questions about how his body works. You can show him you are proud of him by complimenting him for something he does well.

3. Husbands—choose one of the elements of the Love Combination to practice this week. You can make her feel important with your words. You can take all night for foreplay—rub her back, put on her favorite music, kiss her entire body, use your imagination. You can suggest a friendship activity to do together or volunteer to help out with a project you usually do not do.

4. Go away for 24 hours to discuss what you would like to do this year in your sexual interaction. Discuss preferences and creative expressions. Set an atmosphere of acceptance and safety. You want to explore possibilities not establish expectations. Agree ahead of time that you will do only those things you both agree with and that you will not judge each other for saying, "No," to activities you are uncomfortable with. The discussion is one of the most intimate experiences you can engage in, so don't rush it or put pressure on yourselves to do it perfectly. Just share together.

5. Pray together before and after you engage in a sexual experience.

Passion in the Pews

On a church leadership blog, Brandon O'Brian discusses the results of a healthy view of red-hot monogamy: "Relevant Church's sex [sermon] campaign resulted in a 15 percent increase in attendance...New Direction Christian Church conducted its own '40 Nights of Grrreat Sex' program. The pastoral staff handed out daily planners with suggestions for mixing things up. They set up a blog so members could ask questions—and presumably offer advice—anonymously. I hope they also have plans to increase their children's ministry budget in the coming months."[14]

Bill and I also have a collection of e-mailed pictures of babies that have resulted from couples doing the eight-week passion challenge in *Red-Hot Monogamy.*

ABOVE THE LINE

BELOW THE LINE

Three men went golfing together. As they were teeing up at the sixth hole, one of them said to his friends, "It's great to be here with you guys, but I have to tell you that this has cost me in a big way."

"What do you mean?" his friends asked.

"I had to promise my wife that we would remodel the kitchen for the privilege of being here today."

Another of the men jumped in, "Yeah, me too. I had to promise my wife we would landscape the backyard."

For the next couple of holes, these two men lamented the real cost of this golf match. The third man was strangely quiet as they bantered back and forth. Eventually they asked him, "So, how about you? How did you work it out to be here golfing?"

He turned to his friends and said, "I woke up at five this morning and said to my wife, 'Intercourse or golf course?' She said to me, 'Take your jacket.'"

Chapter 7

Activating the Alarms

"The fruit of the Spirit is...joy..."

There is plenty of evidence around us that life is a challenge and that we all must be alert to the potential pitfalls that reside in each of our lives. For instance, there is mounting evidence that we are a sleep-deprived, tired people. One study estimates that over the past century a person's average nightly sleeping time has been reduced by two hours.[15] Seven out of ten Americans suffer from sleep deprivation.[16] According to the National Sleep foundation, "Before Thomas Edison's invention of the light bulb, people slept an average of 10 hours a night; today Americans average 6.9 hours of sleep on weeknights and 7.5 hours per night on weekends."[17]

One Sunday, our pastor, in the middle of his sermon, declared, "The world is run by tired people and Starbucks." Some people laughed while others sighed in resigned agreement. It was more evidence that people are looking for the energy they need to function at work and love their families. You know you might be a coffee addict if:

- You grind your coffee beans in your mouth.
- You have to watch videos in fast-forward.
- The only time you're standing still is during an earthquake.
- You chew on other people's fingernails.
- You can jump-start your car without cables.

- Instant coffee takes too long.
- You short out motion detectors.
- Your first-aid kit contains two pints of coffee with an I.V. hookup.
- You jog to work and arrive yesterday.
- You personally account for more than 1% of the Gross National Product of Brazil.[18]

Alarms sound in your life when things are not right and joy is being threatened. The alarms go off because something is out of balance or some sensitive area of life has been bruised. Your ability to listen to the alarms is one of the keys to a secure and successful marriage.

ALARM 1: INTERRUPTED MOTIVATION

You have been made according to a remarkable blueprint. Even though you have much in common with everyone else, you are still unique. You have a unique appearance, unique DNA, unique fingerprints, and a unique voice print. In the same way, your marriage is unique, even though it has much in common with every other marriage. One of the most fascinating areas of uniqueness is the combination of motivational styles that exists in your relationship.

It began with your courtship. You were attracted to each other and found each other fascinating, though why this was so was probably a mystery to you. This is one of the most asked questions and it has many versions. "How do I know when I have met the right one?" "How did you know he was the one?" "Why did you commit to marry her?" "What was different about her than the other women you dated?"

The answer to these questions is impossible to fully explain, but your motivational style is one of the characteristics that brought you together. You have a certain way you approach life, but you have an inward sense that your approach is not complete. You trust the way you orchestrate your life, but you long for the part of life that you do not have naturally. As a result, you are romantically attracted to people who have what you do not have when it comes to motivational style.

You most likely, therefore, married someone with a different motivational style than yours. This creates an interesting dynamic. When it's time to make a decision, you will both approach the decision with your motivational styles. If your style gets overrun or ignored, the alarm will sound. You may be upset or frustrated or just plain tired, but the alarm will sound.

Let's take a few pages to describe what we mean by motivational styles. There are four basic ones: The Decision-Maker, the Inspirer, the Peacekeeper, and the Policy Holder. You will notice that we illustrate these styles with the way they approach money. We do this for two reasons. First, money is a highly emotional issue that causes many problems for married couples. Your ability to cooperate financially is one of the vital areas of stability that allows you to keep your motivation high. Second, we will be presenting a financial plan in the next chapter that incorporates your motivational styles. We want to get you thinking about how your style affects your financial decisions before we have you work through your plan.

The Decision-Maker

If you are a decision-maker, you gain motivation through being in control of decisions that affect your life. You do not need to be in control of everything, although many people accuse you of being controlling; you just need to have a say in the decisions that impact you. It started early in life. You were born to be in charge of something, but you were too young to be the leader. Something in you drove you to have an opinion on almost everything, and you felt free to share your opinion. Life has always been pretty clear to you, and you have consistently believed that your perspective on life was the best perspective. When others disagree with you, you are confused because you know your outlook is the correct one. If others would just follow you, they would see that you had it figured out from the beginning.

Some might refer to you as a control freak, but chances are you are just more decisive than others. Just to make sure you have not crossed the line from being in charge to needing control, ask yourself:

Guys, is this you?

> Ralph: "Knock knock."
>
> Sally: "Who's there?"
>
> Ralph: "Control freak. Now *you* say 'Control freak who?'"
>
> Or does your TV remote have a PIN access code?

Yes, buddy, you might be a control freak.

Ladies, is this you?

> You want to make mad passionate love to your husband on the floor—just so the bedspread doesn't get wrinkled.
>
> Or you'd love to go on a midnight moonlight sleigh ride with your honey—but only if they let you drive!

Yep, you might be a control freak.

Uncomfortable Confidence

Your natural confidence can make people uncomfortable, but it is an effective asset, especially in the area of finance. Major innovations and breakthroughs in medicine, science, business, and media have happened because someone who was confident with money said yes to an idea and turned the dream into reality.

You might be misunderstood for your boldness and hands-on approach, but keep using the way you are wired for good. You are just naturally confident and do not mind making decisions and taking appropriate risks.

When it comes to money, you naturally believe you ought to be in charge of the financial decisions in your family. You may not want to manage the day-to-day functions of your budget, but you do want to make the decisions that determine the financial direction of your family. The financial gift you bring to your marriage is your clarity. The future looks clear to you, and the path you ought to walk to get there is equally clear. Things are so clear to you that you can make financial decisions with confidence and authority. Your spouse finds this attractive when things are going well.

As with all gifts, this one has a dark side. Your decision-making confidence is so high that you often make decisions without consulting the other people who are affected by the decision. Your spouse periodically finds out after the fact that a financial commitment has been made. You are sorry that the surprise was hard for your spouse to adjust to, but you are still convinced you made the right decision. Most of the time, you believe time will heal whatever misunderstanding exists because eventually your spouse will catch up with your insight and agree that your decision was the best one.

You bring a lot of momentum to your marriage. You recognize opportunity, and you are willing to work hard to make things happen. You have natural talent in making decisions and recognizing effective risks. You also have the capacity to grow in this ability to the point that you can be unusually skilled in expanding your influence.

Tackling Turmoil

At the same time, you can bring turmoil to your marriage because you tend to resist collaboration on decisions. The process of checking with your spouse frustrates you because it slows down the decision. Since the decision seems so obvious to you, it drives you crazy to share your idea, give your spouse time to process it, and then come to a mutual conclusion. You would rather just make the decision yourself, deal with the fallout, and move on.

The other reason you can bring turmoil to your marriage is you may lack restraint. Once you become convinced something needs to be done, you are all go. You want to move fast and will ignore the perspective of other people as you leverage the family budget by making unilateral commitments.

The natural confidence and clear vision you possess is an attractive trait in your spouse's eyes as long as you keep it in check. If you are not careful, this same trait will build resentment in your family. They will feel leveraged or painted into a corner. Resistance to your decision will make him or her look like the "bad guy." For example, you boldly step out to sponsor three teens to attend summer camp. It is a noble cause, but your family now has less of a margin in your budget, which makes your spouse nervous. To say no to you though might make him or her look like a tightwad to the youth pastor or to your own teen kids who are aware of the commitment you made. So your mate goes along with the decision but feels used, marginalized, or devalued. Those feelings, if experienced repeatedly, do not make for a marriage of red-hot monogamy!

> Leverage is important in business, politics, and community organizations because it is impossible to get large groups of people to agree, but nobody likes to feel leveraged in their personal life.

Leverage is important in business, politics, and community organizations because it is impossible to get large groups of people to agree, but nobody likes to feel leveraged in their personal life. Leverage diminishes intimacy because it triggers the fear of being abandoned or rejected in those who are affected by it. This fear then leads to worry, and worry silently erodes relationships.

If you are the worrier, you will lack peace, which puts you on edge more easily. You will not enjoy the moment you are in because you are preoccupied with the future, and the future feels like impending doom. One would think that financial stability (just making more money) would be enough to counteract the fear. It might help, but if the fear is deep enough (as it often is if you were raised in poverty or if you have suffered a severe financial setback), even a sizable savings account won't be enough to stop you from worrying. We need to attack worry at its core and replace it with God's peace.

> Peace is the conclusion that God has His eye on my life and is committed to taking care of me.

Peace is the conclusion that God has His eye on my life and is committed to taking care of me. Peace accompanied by being aware of each other's financial personalities will reconnect you emotionally and will create a workable financial future. One that will keep you both energized and on track.

What Energizes

Decision-makers are energized by:

- Quick financial decisions
- Opportunities that increase personal influence
- The first and the final word in financial decisions
- A cooperative financial environment (I make the decision and you cooperate)
- Financial commitments that are not challenged
- Accurate information at their fingertips so a fast, effective decision can be made

Decision-makers are frustrated by:

- Financial decisions that move slowly
- Long discussions about finances
- Rigid budgets
- Fear of spending money
- Small financial goals
- Criticism about financial decisions they made

The Inspirer

If you love to inspire people, you gain motivation by making other people feel happier. You love to host events that make people laugh or cry about sentimental things or just plain enjoy themselves. You love to give gifts if it makes people smile. You love to send encouraging e-mails, especially when you get a response. As a result, you thrive on attention from others because it confirms to you that you have touched their lives.

You were born with a light-hearted attitude, and you have always longed to be in front of people. You may have been overwhelmed by the stage early in life because it was so important to you. As you have grown, you have become comfortable with the spotlight, and you function well there. You know how to receive attention without getting proud. You can have the focus on you without becoming self-absorbed. The more attention you get, the more confident you are that you are making a real difference in people's lives.

> If you love to inspire people, you gain motivation by making other people feel happier.

You, therefore, spend money to make people happier. It is vital to you that there is room in the budget to host social gatherings, buy encouraging gifts, and do for others what makes them smile. You don't want to ignore the realities of your budget, but if there isn't room in the budget for the activities that produce smiles, you will grow bored with the financial side of life. Once boredom sets in, you are likely to ignore the budget and spend money to recover the inspiration. You will do well not to underestimate the influence of boredom on your financial decisions.

Organizing the Fun

It is likely that you will be reasonable about social expenditures if there is room in your budget for them. If there is not room on paper, you will probably spend the money anyway and trust that things will work out. Truth be told, you don't really like budgets. They are boring and tedious and feel like handcuffs to your creativity. You are glad you are married to someone who tracks money well because you would find it agonizing if you had to balance the checkbook, track your spending, and plan your expenditures. You find life fascinating and highly value the ability to be spontaneous and to take advantage of fun opportunities as they arise.

Your spouse probably loves being with you and is irritated with you all at the same time. You bring a lot more fun to life than your mate ever even imagined, and you bring more financial surprises to life than he or she would ever have allowed.

I (Bill) know this true in my life. I am a peacekeeper by nature and like to manage money to maintain the lowest level of stress possible. This trait is very stable, but it does not inspire anyone. Pam has brought much needed creativity to my life. I have experienced more lifelong memories because of Pam's instincts for valuable life experiences than I could ever have discovered on my own. At the same time, I am periodically surprised by financial commitments she makes. In my mind, we ought to talk about all of these decisions ahead of time. In her frame of reference, she recognizes the opportunity and the way it will enhance our lives, so she does not hesitate. Looking back at our life together, I have to admit that she has been right most of the time, but that doesn't change the fact that it has been irritating.

I Love Spontaneity

It is true that I (Pam) love spontaneity, and I have discovered a few questions that help me keep generosity in perspective:

- If I provide this, will I be robbing others from trusting God to provide? Relying on God is an exhilarating experience, and I would hate to think that others lost their opportunity because of my spur-of-the-moment gift.
- Is there a nonmonetary way to express the same love?
- Have I offered to brainstorm with the ones I am trying to help so they can work toward their own solution?
- Do I really have the money to do this, not from my point of view but from Bill's?

Inspirers are energized by:

- Fun financial decisions
- Opportunities that increase social influence
- Spontaneity in financial decisions
- A festive financial environment

- Financial commitments that leave room for memorable experiences
- Freedom to give to those they love

Inspirers are frustrated by:

- Financial decisions that are inflexible
- Long discussions about finances
- Budgets that never change
- Emotional resistance to spending money
- Long-term financial goals
- Criticism about the cost of social events
- A budget with no flex room for spontaneous giving opportunities

The Peacekeeper

Some of you have the amazing ability to maintain an easy-going, laid-back approach to life. You do not stress over very many things. You have no trouble relaxing, and you are very good at not overcommitting yourself. In fact, you are much better at deciding what you will not do than what you will do.

If you are a peacekeeper, it is clear what you *should not* spend money on, but you have always had trouble coming up with ideas of what you *ought to* spend money on. For this reason, you like a simple approach to life. You are content to work a steady schedule with a steady paycheck. You could settle into a predictable routine in which you go to work at the same time every day, pay the same bills every month at the same time, and avoid financial risks for the duration of your adult life. You prefer this because it keeps stress low.

Your spouse probably fell in love with you because you have such an easy approach to life. Your stress free approach and simple expectations had a calming influence on him or her. Everything just seemed easier when you were around. This caused your spouse's confidence to rise, and he or she began to consider new possibilities. These new opportunities cost money, so financial commitments naturally follow. The more your money is committed the less you like it. You would prefer to have a simple, easy money management system that you set up once and simply run for the rest of your life. You know this is unrealistic, but it is still what you prefer.

Resist Resentment

As a result, you have probably taken steps to trust your more extroverted spouse with your financial goals and then have grown in your resentment toward him or her. It appears to you that there is no rhyme or reason to your spouse's financial moves. You used to think he was bold and aggressive. Now you think he is out of control. You used to believe she was courageous and strong in faith, but now you fight against the conclusion that she is run by her whims. The only outcome you can now see is financial disaster, but you lack the personal energy to confront your spouse. So you silently hope God will intervene and protect your money from your spouse's seemingly emotional decisions.

If you are a peacekeeper, it is clear what you *should not* spend money on, but you have always had trouble coming up with ideas of what you *ought to* spend money on.

Those who are married to a peacekeeper have to choose to not take advantage of their spouse's easygoing nature. Your mild-mannered spouse will give you freedom to spend as you like, but the calm, peaceful demeanor doesn't necessarily mean agreement or acceptance. He may be just fine with things or he may silently argue with you. If he disagrees, he will either grow passive or resentful.

Both of these scenarios will drive you crazy because you like action. The passive response will make you think he doesn't care. The resentment you will probably never see coming until he or she blows a gasket on you or simply walks out one day with bags packed and a note that reads, "I just couldn't take it anymore." The peacekeeper will not demand to be involved in the financial process, so be careful to keep your diplomatic spouse active in your money decisions.

Peacekeepers are energized by:

- A respectful financial environment (everyone involved is as important as everyone else involved)
- Simple financial decisions
- Opportunities that make life easier
- Predictability in financial decisions
- Financial commitments that create margin in the budget
- Predictable earning plan

Peacekeepers are frustrated by:

- Financial decisions that are not well thought out
- Random discussions about finances
- Budgets that are ignored
- Lack of restraint in spending money
- Financial goals that are ignored
- Criticism about being cautious
- Work that pays randomly, on commission, or freelance income that is erratic

The Policy Holder

The final motivational style is based on the love for doing things right. Some of you believe there is a right way to do things and a wrong way to do things. You function best when life is in order. If you have your way, your office is in order, your home is in order, your closet is in order, and your finances are in order. You love budgets, money management systems, and spreadsheets. You wholeheartedly agree with financial presenters who say, "You need to have a family budget, and you need to stick to it. You should track your spending for a month. Save every receipt and write down every expenditure. That way you will know exactly where your money is going."

The gift you bring to your marriage financially is your ability to organize and handle the details of your money plan. You find joy in creating the budget and planning out your financial purchases. For you, the budget is king. If you are a policy holder, you wrote the budget so you would have a plan, and

> If you are a policy holder, you wrote the budget so you would have a plan, and you expect that you and your spouse will follow the plan to the letter.

you expect that you and your spouse will follow the plan to the letter. You believe every detail of the plan, and you feel good about life when the plan is honored and followed.

Can't We Just Work Together?

On the other hand, you are confused when the plan is ignored. You are frustrated that all the effort you put into planning the budget has been disregarded. Since your spouse does not take the same care with the budget that you do, you consistently evaluate the process. Some days you think that you are over thinking, and you tell yourself to lighten up. On other days, you struggle with anger toward your spouse because you feel like the budget is a lie. You ask yourself, "Why did we spend all this time working on a budget if we are just going to pitch it out the window?" "Why did my spouse say he was going to follow this when he didn't really mean it?" "Why would she lie to me by saying that she was going to work together with me on this?"

Since you are the organized one in the family, you are probably in charge of organizing the bills and paying your obligations. You took this on with enthusiasm because you sensed that your talents were being respected, but now you are just plain frustrated. You have the responsibility for keeping the budget in order, but the one who helped you set it up is not playing by the rules. You are consistently surprised by money that has been spent, and you feel powerless to do anything about it. You resort to talking, complaining, arguing, and pleading, but nothing ever changes. In frustration, you go back to taking care of things, but you are bored and disappointed. You only hope you don't give up on your spouse one day and ruin what you are trying to build together.

Policy Holders are energized by:

- Thought out financial decisions
- Opportunities that make sense to them
- Predictability in financial decisions
- A precise financial environment (everyone follows the rules)
- Financial commitments that stick to the budget

Policy Holders are frustrated by:

- Financial decisions that change impulsively
- Casual discussions about finances
- Budgets that are violated
- Lack of restraint in spending money
- Financial goals that are ignored
- Criticism about being precise

Decoder Moment: Each of you fill in the blanks:

Wife: I think my financial motivational style is _____

Husband: I think the strength of that style and one benefit to our relationship it provides is _____

Husband: I think my financial motivational style is _____

Wife: I think the strength of that style and one benefit to our relationship it provides is _____

Keep it positive for now; problem solving will come later. Use this time to compliment and build up your mate in the way he or she approaches the funding of your love.

ALARM 2: TOXIC DECISIONS

None of us have experienced perfect lives. Some of you reading this book have had relatively easy lives with few bumps along the road. Some of you had horrendous experiences growing up and have been trying to overcome those influences your entire adult life. Most of you are somewhere in between. You have had your struggles, and you have learned to cope enough to function well at work and in your friendships.

Along the way, we all tend to take some measures to defend our hearts from being broken. It may be as simple as avoiding people who bug us, or we may stay busy so we don't have time to complicate our lives with challenging relationships. There is no need to spend a lot of time and effort analyzing these simple precautions. It is quite possible, however, that you have made one or two toxic decisions along the path that create interruptions in the intimacy of your relationship. These toxic reactions are shrill alarms that sound the need for change, growth, and cooperation.

You don't want to create a toxic relationship like these couples experience:

> A man appears before a judge, asking for a divorce. The judge quietly reviews some papers and then says, "Please tell me why you are seeking a divorce."
>
> "Because," the man says, "I live in a two-story house."
>
> The judge replies, "What kind of a reason is that? What's the big deal about a two-story house?"
>
> "Well, Judge, one story is 'I have a headache,' and the other story is 'It's that time of the month.'"
>
> TOXIC!

■ ■ ■

> A henpecked husband was advised by a psychiatrist to assert himself.

"You don't have to let your wife bully you," he said. "Go home and show her you're the boss!"

The husband decided to take the doctor's advice. He went home, slammed the door, shook his fist in his wife's face, and growled, "From now on you're taking orders from me. I want my supper right now, and when you get it on the table, go upstairs and lay out my clothes. Tonight I am going out with the boys. You're going to stay at home where you belong. Another thing, you know who's going to tie my bow tie?"

"I certainly do," his wife said calmly. "The undertaker."

EXTREMELY TOXIC!

These toxic decisions need to be replaced with ones that promote vulnerability, productivity, and accountability. Consider the examples below of people who made toxic decisions that have insulated them from the people they love the most.

I Won't Be Controlled

Steve—Steve grew up with a mom who was very controlling. She constantly told him what to do, when to do it, how to do it, and what it looked like when it was good enough. This control went way beyond the normal instructions that parents need to give to their children, and it continued well into his early adult years. If he did not respond to her demands, she would use emotional outbursts to get him to comply. She would scream, yell, storm around the house, insult him, and threaten him with public embarrassment. Just before his twentieth birthday, Steve made the conscious decision, "No one will ever control me again."

This was more than a passing statement in reaction to a hard day. It was a decision made deep in his heart that shaped his development from this point forward. In his midtwenties, he fell in love and married a lovely young lady. If you asked Steve today, "Do you love your wife?" he would quickly and emphatically say, "Yes!"

When any conflict arises in their relationship, however, he immediately feels she is trying to control him. He erupts at her with degrading insults. He consistently calls her things that he would never direct at anyone else. She has pleaded with him to stop because she loves him very much. They have been to numerous counselors to adjust Steve's behaviors, all to no avail. Steve has sincerely tried to change, but he is overwhelmed with fear any time he perceives his wife is trying to control. Before he can even think about what he is doing, he begins to berate her. His wife is very frustrated and at a loss over how to connect with the man she loves.

It took years to eventually come to the surface, but Steve finally blurted out that he had decided early in life that no one would ever control him again. If you knew all the situations with his mom, you might conclude this was a necessary decision, but it has sabotaged the ability for anyone to have any real influence in his life. For Steve, the wonderful influence of a loving spouse was an impossibility because he had forever shut himself off from it. For years, he has been afraid of the person he loves the most on earth.

Steve now needs to decide if he wants to hang on to the perceived safety of being emotionally isolated from people or if he wants to give a significant place of influence to his wife. He is afraid to do this because he doesn't understand how to be vulnerable in a safe way. It feels as if he will give control to her and to everyone in his life if he lets down his guard even a little bit. This is not true, of course, but he has relied on his isolation for so long that he cannot picture himself living any different. It feels to him like the biggest step of trust he has ever taken. It feels dangerous and reckless to him, and yet he knows he will lose his wife if he doesn't do it.

> Steve doesn't understand how to be vulnerable in a safe way.

I Won't Get Hurt

Jenny—Jenny's life has been a challenge from the very beginning. Her mom had multiple sexual partners in her early twenties and still isn't sure who Jenny's father is. Mom had many men live with her throughout Jenny's developmental years. Some of them were nice and easy to get along with, but many of them were verbally and physically intimidating. During her high school years, Jenny was pretty much on her own. She had no supervision to speak of and pursued any social activities she desired. Following in her mom's footsteps, she had many sexual partners. Her discernment level left a lot to be desired, and when she was nineteen, three men raped her during an isolated social event.

The pain in Jenny's life forced her to come to some conclusions about herself and about how to live. Her decision was, "I am going to keep everybody at arm's length so I won't get hurt." For a long time, this decision helped her function. She met and married a stable, opinionated man. He was willing to make all the major decisions for the family, provided a stable income, and was predictable in his behavior. She gave birth to two lovely kids and went about the business of living a relatively boring existence. She thought she could keep her emotional needs under wraps throughout her adult life and give herself wholeheartedly to her family.

This worked fine until her youngest child started school. She began to have more free time than she was used to, which gave her plenty of time to reflect on her life. She was gifted with a strong emotional makeup, but it was underdeveloped because it had been stuffed down for so long. Now, her emotional drives began to stir and they were strong.

Because her skills were not equal to the task, she found her heart wandering in an intoxicating web of romantic interludes. She thought she could keep these hidden and under control, but one of them blossomed into an intense attraction. Again, her skills were too weak to do battle with this attraction, so she concluded it was love. She eventually abandoned her husband of 17 years, settled for part-time visitation with her kids, and is desperately trying to make her new relationship work. Her new husband is trying to adjust to her very intense emotional needs, but she believes he can meet them so he carries on.

I Don't Want to Have Issues

Richard—Richard's father was a harsh, hard charging businessman.

He was very demanding of his son and critical of everything he did. His mom was likewise harsh and demanding and demonstrated very little affection. His dad and mom often argued in front of Richard and his brother without resolving their conflicts. Over time, they ignored each other more and more as they sought separate social lives, financial lives, and schedules.

Richard tried dating a few times before he was 21, but none of the relationships went well. Richard found it confusing when the young ladies would bring up issues in their relationship. He didn't understand the issues or the process of trying to resolve them. At the same time, he discovered pornography on the Internet and found that it stirred something within him that was mysterious and satisfying.

When he met Sandy, he thought he finally met a woman with whom he could live. Her needs were remarkably low, and she seemed amazingly easy to get along with. He concluded that he would probably not have any issues with her, or they would at least be rare. He asked Sandy to marry him, and she agreed.

The first couple years of marriage were all right. Richard was pleased that his interest in pornography went down. He, of course, didn't share any of this with Sandy because he hoped the struggle was now a thing of the past.

In time, Sandy started bringing up topics that needed to be discussed. She was concerned that Richard wasn't spending enough time with their kids. She was concerned that Richard didn't have any friends. She thought he was underachieving in his career and could probably do better. She didn't feel as valued as she had when they were newlyweds.

Richard found himself overwhelmed and withdrew emotionally from her. He remembers the day he decided, "It is easier to just view pornography than try to work through all these issues with Sandy." From that day forward, he spent more time alone on the computer and less time with Sandy. They were both hanging on to the relationship for the sake of the kids, but neither of them had a lot of hope for their relationship after the kids grew up. For Richard and Sandy to reconnect and prepare for a future together, Richard needs to decide that the challenge of developing a real relationship is better than the escape of pornography.

I Can Train Him

Gena—Gena's parents were very much in love with each other and were skilled parents. She was encouraged in her pursuits and secure in their love. She concluded that marriage was easy and all she had to do to have a marriage like her parents was to train her husband to be like her dad.

When she met Peter, he was pursuing his master's degree and was well-liked by his peers. He was good at conversation and was quite attracted to Gena. It didn't take long before they were married and pursuing life together. From the beginning, Gena made strong suggestions about how Peter should arrange his clothes, spend his time, sit at the dinner table, act when he got home from work, and so on. All her suggestions were good and well-intentioned, but they were incessant. Many of the areas she had strong opinions about were areas of preference rather than necessity. At first, Peter was flattered by her attention, but he eventually grew tired of the constant demands. He eventually found solace in working long hours away from home.

If Gena wants to discover the type of marriage she had envisioned, she will need to decide to value Peter's opinions more and deliberately take time to consider what he wants in the relationship. She has a strong sense that her perspective is right, so it will take considerable focus for her to value his perspective as much as she values her own.

■■■

Other examples of toxic relationship decisions include:

- "I decided I would never be embarrassed."
- "I decided I would be happy no matter what it took."
- "My career is more important than my relationships."

- "I think I married the wrong person."
- "I will never be like my dad/mom."
- "I can never forgive him/her."

These toxic decisions have the ability to pollute the emotional tone of the marriage and create distance between a husband and wife who could otherwise flourish in their love.

The Game Plan

Unwinding the effects of toxic decisions on your ability to pursue satisfying, enjoyable relationships is much easier to talk about than to implement. These decisions have had profound emotional, social, and spiritual influence on you. These decisions helped you cope with difficult circumstances that involved the most important people in your life at the time. Telling you to just get over them is unrealistic and results only in more pressure and relationship failure. There are steps, however, that you can pursue that will, with time, help you get out from under the tyranny of these toxic decisions:

Step 1: Identify the toxic decision. You cannot replace something you are unaware of. You cannot apply the truth to an area of your life you are deceived about. Bringing destructive behavior to light is the first step to healing. Look over the examples of toxic decisions listed in the section above. Ask yourself, "Have I made any of these?" Are there any other toxic decisions you have become aware of as you have read this chapter?

Step 2: Intellectually choose a response that is different from the one that caused the problem. You may have to brainstorm a little and find three or four possible replacement behaviors before you arrive at one you are willing to implement. Again, this is harder to do than to say. Of course, you want to do things differently. You are tired of hurting the ones you love the most. You are weary of the frustration that hovers in your life as you fail to live out your intentions toward your spouse and children. Intellectually identifying a different way of doing things is not enough to change it because strong emotional forces are at work committing you to the way you have always done things. You cannot move on to the next steps, however, until you choose a different behavior.

Step 3: Commit your new behavior choice to prayer for 30 days. Ask God to alert you when you need to do something different than you normally would. Ask God to give you strength to respond differently. This is a major change, and you will need every resource you can find. You will need the support of your spouse, the encouragement of your friends, and most of all, the spiritual strength that only God can provide.

Step 4: Practice the new intentional behavior. Every time you deliberately practice the replacement actions, your emotional commitment to the new way of doing things grows. You have been emotionally committed to the toxic decision for so long that you are programmed to continue it. It has become ingrained in your routine so that it is now automatic. You don't have to do anything to set it off. It will respond to the right impulse in the twinkle of an eye. It will take you from peace to stress in an instant. You will erupt toward the ones you love before you are even aware there is a problem. You will spend too many days feeling bad for what you have done, apologizing for your actions, then repeating the exact same destruction next time life calls for it.

The only way to make the new behavior a habit is to practice it. Our boys use a phrase in their athletic pursuits that fits here: "If you can do the drill, you can do the skill." You will certainly not be very proficient at first, but the more you deliberately practice the new skill, the more natural it will become for you.

It's Time for Practice

Disarming your reactions will take time and practice. It is wise to picture your new reaction next time the old patterns are triggered. Athletes picture their success ahead of time to get themselves focused. Soldiers create a mental image of their mission long before they ever take to the battlefield so they are not subject to their fears and civilian instincts. Businessmen picture the outcome of negotiations before the meeting to develop a mindset of confidence. Personal growth works the same way. Success that is pictured ahead of time is more likely to become a reality.

Deliberately attempt your new behavior as soon as you are aware that the old patterns have been triggered. Don't worry about being awkward at this moment. You may have to say something like, "I was about to say something stupid, so I'm going to say nothing until I count to 20. Then I'm going to try to say what I really want to say." You may even have to say to the one you love, "I don't know how to react right now. If I follow my instincts, I'm sure I will do the wrong thing again. What would you do right now if you were in my shoes?"

Let's use Gena as an example. Her confidence causes her to have an opinion about most everything. Her opinionated nature makes her impatient with indecisive situations. It drives her crazy when issues are left unresolved for very long or if someone hesitates to make a decision. As a result, she is quick to make decisions in her life before other people can evaluate her. She also makes decisions for people if they hesitate to reach a conclusion that is obvious to her. This encompasses most situations in life since she considers most situations to be obvious.

Step 1 for Gena is to identify that her impatience with others is toxic to her relationships. People grow passive around her because they believe she will make all the decisions anyway. They then grow in their resentment toward her since they no longer feel that they are equal players in whatever pursuit they are engaged in.

Step 2 for Gena is to decide a different course of action. She knows she cannot become indecisive because this would go against everything she knows to be true about herself. She was born to be a leader and to be a strong decision-maker. She can, however, approach decisions differently. She concludes it would be a good idea to ask, "Is this my responsibility?" Her instincts told her that everything was her responsibility, but she thought that was probably not true. It may seem simple to others, but this was a monumental choice for her. She concluded that she should be decisive about anything that was her responsibility, but she should leave the rest of life alone. She intellectually knew this was correct, but all her instincts argued with her conclusion.

Step 3 for Gena is to commit this to prayer. She could ask God for the wisdom to clearly identify the areas of life she was responsible for. She could also ask for the same clarity to identify the areas of life that need to be left to others.

Step 4 for Gena is to proactively ask, "Is this my responsibility? If it is, make the decision. If it is not, leave it alone." She can practice this in the mirror, while she walks, and in her personal prayer time. She can also practice it as she goes through her daily routine. The real test will come the next time someone is slow to make a decision in an area she has no real responsibility for. She knows that her instincts are going to scream at her to do something even though she knows she should not give in.

Decoder Moment: Your Game Plan

Take a few minutes to identify your game plan for unwinding a toxic decision in your life:

Step 1: Each of you answer this question:

I feel most out of control in our life when _____ _____ (insert example), and when I feel out of control I think I _____ (insert behavior).

That behavior became toxic when I _____ _____ (insert a time you felt you might not have handled your feelings well). I'm sorry I resorted to this behavior, and I'm asking you to forgive me.

(Example: I feel most out of control in our life when *we don't have enough money for basics,* and when I feel out of control I think I *start working overtime and tighten all spending.*

That behavior became toxic when I *belittled you about your contribution.* I'm sorry I resorted to this behavior, and I'm asking you to forgive me.

Step 2: Different courses of action I could take rather than what I normally do:

Idea 1

Idea 2

Idea 3

Step 3: Pray about your new plan for 30 days.

Date I will begin praying:

Date I will move from prayer to action:

Step 4: Choose one of the ideas and write down two or three ways to practice this new behavior.

Practice Plan 1

Practice Plan 2

Practice Plan 3

When the alarms sound in your relationship, it's time to huddle together and go into action.

 UNLOCKING THE CODE:

Dinner and Dialogue for a Heart-to-Heart Connection

On a date this week, each of you surrender one past decision or action and share with your mate a new choice you are making that will be more healthy for your relationship. When your spouse shares avoid saying:

- "I told you so."
- "About time!"

- "That's not the only thing!"
- "Is that all you can think of?"

Instead say, "Thanks for sharing that. Thanks for working on our relationship to make it better for both of us."

■■■

We're all imperfect:

> A young couple were on their honeymoon. The husband was sitting in the bathroom on the edge of the bathtub saying to himself, "How can I tell my wife that I've got really smelly feet and that my socks stink? I've managed to keep it from her while we were dating, but she's bound to find out sooner or later that my feet stink. How do I tell her?"
>
> Meanwhile, the wife was sitting on the bed saying to herself, "How do I tell my husband that I've got really bad breath? I've been very lucky to keep it from him while we were courting, but as soon as he's lived with me for a week, he's bound to find out. How do I tell him gently?"
>
> The husband finally plucked up enough courage to tell his wife. He walked into the bedroom and over to the bed. He climbed over to his wife, put his arm around her neck, moved his face close to hers, and said, "Darling, I have a confession to make."
>
> "So have I, love," she said.
>
> "Don't tell me, you've eaten my socks."

ABOVE THE LINE

BELOW THE LINE

There is an urban legend about a huge wedding with about 300 guests. At the reception, the groom got up on stage at the microphone to talk to the crowd. He said he wanted to thank everyone for coming, many from long distances, to support them at their wedding. He especially wanted to thank both families for coming and to thank his new father-in-law for providing such a fabulous reception. He thanked everyone for bringing gifts, and he said he wanted to give everyone a special gift just from him. So, taped to the bottom of everyone's chair, including the wedding party, was a manila envelope. He said this was his gift and told everyone to open the envelopes.

Inside each envelope was an 8x10 picture of his best man in a compromising position with the bride. Seems he had gotten suspicious that the two of them were having an affair and hired a private detective to trail them for weeks. After he stood there and watched the people's reactions for a couple of minutes, he turned to the best man and his own bride and said his final good-bye, then walked out on the dumbfounded crowd.

He had the marriage annulled first thing that Monday morning.

Chapter 8

Golden Goals

"The fruit of the Spirit is...goodness..."

We finally got a GPS. When we were growing up, a Global Positioning System was something reserved for the military, aviation, and boat captains. The idea of a satellite system telling you where you were was reserved for the most sophisticated and deep-pocketed among us. It was awesome to read about, but it all seemed a little too James Bond to ever be part of our daily reality.

Then we heard that pets could be implanted with devices that could link to a GPS so that if Fido ever got lost, you could find him and ask, "What were you thinking? Why would you want to wander away from the people who love and feed you every day?"

Then we bought a car that could be outfitted with a security system that worked off a GPS. If anyone ever stole our car, we could call a number that would activate the system. The satellites would find our car and lead the police right to the thief.

And now we have a GPS that travels with us and helps us find our destinations. There are three reasons why we love our GPS: (1) It has a bigger view of life than we do. From its position in space, the satellite can see where we've been, where we're going, and the best route to get there. (2) It gives specific directions for the journey. Our device never tells us to simply turn and hope we can figure out which direction. It tells us which way to turn and when to turn. (3) It helps us get back on track when we're lost. If we take a wrong turn, or if we ignore the system for a while, it will recalibrate the route and lead us along a new path to the same destination.

As you pursue your life together, you need to develop your own GPS to navigate the productive side of life.

The Mission

Your life is going to cost you a small fortune. Your house costs money, your kids cost money, your mistakes cost money, and your cars cost money. To keep up with the never-ending spending, you must commit to earn a living. As a result, significant questions about careers take center stage for every couple at various times. The ability to decipher the best course of action for each spouse sets the couple free to stay in love. Competition over the plan for your careers erodes love and shuts the vault of your heart toward one another.

> Your life is going to cost you a small fortune.

A couple's success is, therefore, tied to their ability to answer questions such as, "What career is best for me? What career is best for my spouse? How do we coordinate our careers so our goals for our family are attained? What balance of time at work and time with each other will maximize our ability to provide for the ones we love?"

Designed to Work

Every one of us was designed for work. In chapter 3, we talked about the fact that you, and everyone in your family, were given a unique ability that is effective and influential. One of the reasons this talent was given to you was so that you could build a career that is successful enough to provide for your family and significant enough to provide a sense of purpose when your family has been raised.

I (Bill) vividly remember in early adulthood the captivating allure of a career. Pam and I married when we were twenty years old. The responsibility level in my life instantly intensified. I can still picture the thoughts that drove me during those newlywed days:

- I love this woman as I have never loved anyone.

- I want her to be proud of me.

- We have bills.

- I need to figure out how to do something I love and make enough money to take care of us.

Based on my need, I committed to a bachelor's degree and then a master's degree in theology because I figured out that I loved ministry. An initial confidence set in, and I pursued these goals with fervor and diligence. I committed to the first steps in my career and felt good about what I was doing.

Then Pam and I had kids. A whole new set of thoughts entered into my experience:

- I love these kids more than I ever imagined.

- I am willing to do whatever it takes to care for these little people.

- These boys sure can eat!

- How do they manage to break everything they get a hold of?

- What were they thinking when they did that?

- I love what I do, but somehow I need to make more money doing this.

A New Gear

I kicked into a different gear and worked hard. I worked as a pastor, drew house plans on the side to keep up with the financial challenge, and dreamed of the future. I truly believed we were in sync with life and that I had discovered God's plan for our life.

Then we had our third and final son. It was subtle at first, but by the time our youngest was two, Pam's intensity about her career was burning brightly. I wanted Pam to succeed, but I didn't want her success to interfere with my success. For the first time in my life, I started to feel as if I were competing with Pam. I had assumed that we were working off the same page. My goals were her goals. My success was her goal. Intellectually, I knew she would one day pursue her own goals, but I was not aware that it would infringe on my ability to fully commit to my career.

A different and surprising set of thoughts now clouded my mind:

- I still love this woman more than anyone I have ever met.

- She is incredibly talented.

- I can't believe I am now competing with her for time and opportunity.

- I think she has more energy than I do. Will I be able to maintain a successful path with her being so intent about her career?

- How will our kids do if we both get as busy as I have been?

- I hope Pam doesn't turn out to be as controlling as my mom was.

Looking back, Pam's pursuit of her career was not nearly as threatening to my career as I imagined, but it sure seemed like it at the time. I argued with Pam a lot during those years because I thought I needed to keep her commitments balanced. I even thought to myself, *I need to stand her down at least once a year so her pursuits do not take over our life.*

As I look back, I know that my reaction was way overstated. Pam and I have developed a writing and speaking ministry that we both enjoy. Pam is far better at marketing and networking than I could ever be. She has a higher confidence level than I do when it comes to believing that people want to hear our message. She is very talented at managing life from the road in a freelance lifestyle.

We knew we were going to have to develop a plan if we were going to stay above the line where success and security are preserved. We both wanted to enhance our careers and our love without entering into a competition with each other.

PRODUCTION STEP 1: SET GOALS

It is good to work according to God's design for you as an individual and it is good to be as productive as you can be. In writing to his friends in the city of Philippi, the apostle Paul revealed the focus and intensity of his goal, "I press on to take hold of that for which Christ Jesus took hold of me…Forgetting what is behind and straining toward what is ahead, I press on toward the

> You may not be able to articulate your purpose in life or discern your destiny, but you can identify what you are supposed to do next.

goal to win the prize for which God has called me heavenward in Christ Jesus" (Philippians 3:12-14). Paul was not passive about his pursuits, he pressed on. He did not wait around for things to happen, he pressed on.

An effective goal can be recognized because it SNAPS. It is **S**pecific, it asks, "What is **N**ext?" it is **A**djustable, it reflects your **P**ace, and it is based on your **S**kills:

Specific. Effective goals are specific. "We want to get closer this year" is a good desire, but it is a vague goal. It's hard to know when you are as close as you were hoping. It's better to make your goal specific, such as: "We will go on a date every week this year," or "We will both write down 10 questions we would like to talk about that do not include work or financial responsibilities."

Next. Effective goals answer the question, "What is next?" Since goals are designed to keep us in motion, their primary purpose is to help us figure out what is next in our lives. You may not be able to articulate your purpose in life or discern your destiny, but you can identify what you are supposed to do next.

Adjustable. Effective goals are flexible. You are interested in doing well in life, but no one knows the future. Setting goals does not require you to know exactly how things will turn out. Goals were designed to keep us in motion so God could lead us in His plan for our lives. You do not need to know exactly where you will end up. You simply need to choose a direction and tell God you will cooperate with Him if He changes directions with you. We believe this is the intent of Proverbs 16:9,

> In his heart a man plans his course,
>   but the LORD determines his steps.

It is our job to plan our way. It is God's job to direct our steps.

Paced. Effective goals can be pursued at your pace. Goals that push you to move beyond your pace will bring fatigue. Goals that slow you down below your pace will do the same thing. When you find goals you can work on at your best pace, you will find them fulfilling and energizing.

Skill-based. Effective goals reflect your unique ability. Every goal you set that is based on the talent you do best will be relatively effort-less and will have a bigger impact than the other things you do.

EVIDENCE COLLECTION:

Answer the following questions and share your answers with your spouse:

- What career step do I want to take this year?

- How does this step reflect my unique ability? (Is it something God has called me to in my skill set, talent, and passion?)

- How does this step match my pace? (Will it speed up our life? If so, for how long? Will it slow down our life? If so, for how long?)

- How will this step affect our marriage and family? (Will I gain more time or less time with my mate, children, and extended family?)

What career step do I want to take in the next five years?

- How does this step reflect my unique ability?
- How does this step match my pace?
- How will this step affect our marriage and family?

PRODUCTION STEP 2:
EVALUATE BASED ON PRIORITIES

Every activity and commitment in your life can be assigned a priority. You have A priorities that are the "musts." You have B priorities that are important to you because they enhance your life, but they are not as interesting to you nor is it essential that they get done. You also have C priorities that you would like to accomplish, but they are not absolutely necessary or they have more flexible timelines.

A problem arises when there is not enough time or resources to accomplish all of them. If you do not have a strong sense of your priorities, everything feels just as important as everything else. That's not a problem if you have only four or five responsibilities to take care of, but if that were the case, you wouldn't be married, you certainly wouldn't have children, and you would be isolated from people.

If you merge all your priorities, you will have one of two reactions. You will either be lethargic or overactive. You may conclude that it is impossible to do everything you need to do at the level you think it should be done. This scenario will discourage you and lead you to inactivity, or you may attack your responsibilities in a frenzied attempt to do everything perfectly. Since this is impossible, you will drive everyone around you crazy with expectations as you recruit them to assist you in accomplishing the impossible.

The problem is not that you think everything is important. It's that you think everything is just as important as everything else. The purpose for having priorities is to budget your effort. Your A priorities deserve the best you have to give. You should be willing to stretch yourself for these goals, work hard at these goals, and sacrifice other areas of life to accomplish them. B priorities should get good effort from you but nowhere near the effort you put into your A priorities. C priorities ought to get what you have

> Your A priorities deserve the best you have to give.

left. These activities do not need to be done at a high level, and they may not need to be done at all. You are free to decide what "barely acceptable" looks like and work these priorities accordingly.

When you tenaciously put effort into your commitments based on their priority level, you discover the kind of satisfaction that comes from knowing that the most important things in your life are flourishing.

EVIDENCE COLLECTION:

Prioritize each aspect of your career listed below.
Use a different color pen for each of you.

A B C I want to work full-time for a company.

A B C I want to work for a company but telecommute from a home office.

A B C I want to work part-time.

A B C I want a regulated schedule.

A B C I want to own my own business.

A B C I want a steady paycheck.

A B C I want freedom to make financial decisions without a lot of conversation with others.

A B C I want health insurance to be included in my compensation.

A B C I want a retirement plan to be included in my compensation.

A B C I want to work hard on my career when our kids are young.

A B C I want to work hard on my career when our kids are teenagers.

A B C I want to work hard on my career after our kids leave home.

A B C I want to retire early.

A B C I never want to retire (possibly change careers or down-scale hours, but I love to work).

PRODUCTION STEP 3: BALANCE YOUR CAREERS

Do you remember the conversations early in your marriage when you asked, "What would you like for dinner tonight, honey?"

"I don't know. What are our options?"

"Well, let's see. We can feast on tuna casserole. We can indulge ourselves on hot dogs and beans. Or we can delight ourselves with leftover spaghetti. What's your pleasure?"

Many couples look back on their early days together as some of the most memorable, significant, and impoverished times of their life. We reminisce about the lean days and we laugh when we remember how creative we had to be to make our few dollars stretch as far as possible. None of us, however, want to spend our entire lives financially challenged.

> Many couples look back on their early days together as some of the most memorable, significant, and impoverished times of their life.

Each of you was created to be productive. It began with Adam and Eve when "the LORD God took the man and put him in the Garden of Eden to work it and take care of it" (Genesis 2:15). It was the first couple's job to cultivate the garden so it would be more productive and not get overrun by overgrowth or weeds. It required both creativity and problem-solving, and it was exactly what they were created for.

The account of the tower of Babel gives us a notable example of the remarkable talent that God placed in the human race. The context is certainly negative, but the reality is that mankind is incredibly creative, capable, and innovative. Even though God could not endorse the project, even He acknowledged the high level of skill that was inherent in men and women. "But the LORD came down to see the city and the tower that the men were building. The LORD said, 'If as one people speaking the same language they have begun to do this, then nothing they plan to do will be impossible for them'" (Genesis 11:5-6).

> One of the great challenges you face is to balance your pursuits so that both of you make your contribution to life and your relationship flourishes.

You and your spouse are both gifted. You have a contribution to make, and it will demand expression amidst the challenges of your life. You discovered each other because you found something in each other that was attractive. You somehow came to the conclusion that you could build your lives together. As you have found out, it is harder to do than to dream about. One of the great challenges you face is to balance your pursuits so that both of you make your contribution to life and your relationship flourishes.

I (Pam) am concerned about the number of women who are walking away from good, stable men who are good providers, diligent fathers, and caring husbands. These men are often not romantic in the romance novel sense of flowers, candy, and amorous pleasures. Sometimes men express romance differently. They build you a home, making sure the kitchen window faces the backyard so you can see the kids play. They buy you a new set of tires for Christmas so you are safe on the road.

While we encourage these husbands to read our book *Red-Hot Monogamy* and to build those romantic muscles, we also want to caution women from walking away from good men into the arms of a smooth talker. If he can smooth talk you, he can just as easily smooth talk another woman in a few years when he's done playing with you.

The key to unlocking love when married to "a good, stable man" is to know the legend on the map of his heart. The following symbols may just be his way of trying to express romance:

- Painting the house means "I am proud to be your husband, and I want you to be proud to live in the home I can provide."

- Mowing the lawn means "I want you to have Saturdays to be with our family, so I'll handle the yard."

- Working long hours means "I think you are one amazing woman, and I want you and the kids to have the best life offers."

Both husband and wife should keep one caution in mind as you develop your careers. When you are making money, it's easy to become independent and walk away if things get tough. According to *Forbes* magazine journalist Michael Noer, career women who make over $30,000 a year are more prone to divorce their husbands.[19] And 70 percent of all divorces are initiated by women, which should cause us to pause and ask ourselves, "Why are so many women feeling the desire to walk out?"[20]

Canadian research reveals a similar trend: women in North America are twice as likely as men to file for divorce. Janis Magnusson, a Calgary divorce mediator, says she frequently sees women with unreal expectations of marriage and their partners. "Women expect a Prince Charming, while men just want a wife, sex, food and a job."[21] To be fair, some women file because it is just one more thing in a list of many the husband won't follow through on. With statistics this high, we women should stop and ask when we are angry, "Am I being unrealistic? Could any man meet the need I am feeling right now, or can only God meet this need?"

Balance Your Pursuits with Prayer

A GPS system needs to connect with a satellite before it can identify your location or effectively plot a course for you to travel. In the same way, you need to connect with the One who has a bird's-eye view of your life. He knows the end from the beginning, and He knows how the events of your life work together. He understands your talents and desires because He created you and He can read your heart. He has also committed to "cause all things to work together for good" in your life as an individual and as a couple (Romans 8:28 NASB). And He has promised to give you great wisdom:

> I will instruct you and teach you in the way you should go;
> I will counsel you and watch over you.
> (Psalm 32:8)

It is widely recognized that couples who pray together regularly have more stable marriages and report a higher satisfaction level than those who do not pray together. One of the main reasons is that there is less conflict over careers when both spouses are seeking the same God for wisdom.

God doesn't stutter and God doesn't play head games. He will never lead your spouse in one direction while He leads you in a contradictory direction. You will recognize a supernatural sense of unity in your pursuits, which will make you more willing to commit to those pursuits while, at the same time, you readily defer to your spouse when his or her career takes center stage.

If you find yourself in competition, begin praying for your mate. Ask God to maximize his or her achievement, potential, and future success. Ask your mate to pray for you also. After praying for one another for a set time (a few weeks or months), regroup and see how God might be moving each of you to a more unified plan. Look for a course you can run in together, or at least in the same direction, so you can maintain the higher goal of a happy, satisfying marriage while pursuing different career paths.

Balance Your Intensity by Interest

Interest in a career varies from duty to a sense of destiny. Some of you work because you have to while others of you work for the sheer joy of accomplishment. Sometimes the satellite signal to your GPS is strong; sometimes the signal is weak.

Similarly, each person has a career "signal." In some people, the signal is strong. In others, the signal is relatively weak. This does not mean that people with a strong career signal are superior; life is much more than just work. Children need to be raised, and they require an enormous investment. Neighborhoods need active citizens who help make the community

> Some of you work because you have to while others of you work for the sheer joy of accomplishment.

function well. Churches need volunteers who give of their time and talents to create an environment of growth and grace.

It is likely that one of you has a stronger career signal than the other. You were created with this strong signal because you are supposed to make an intense commitment to financial productivity and workplace influence. You have a significant contribution to make in the world of work, which may consist of innovation in your field or influence in the lives of people at work. To help you recognize this arena of influence, you have been given a strong desire to work and a large capacity for the demands of a career. It will be best for your marriage if you are able to make a strong commitment to your career. If you have to diminish the signal in your heart, you will grow restless and irritable. You will likely put too much pressure on the members of your family because you will try to work out your desire to produce through their lives.

It is impossible to outline all the possible combinations that exist in a couple's career signals. You may both have strong signals. You may both have weak signals. One of you may have all bars lit while the other has two. The key is to explore the unique blend that exists in your relationship and make career decisions that are consistent with your combination.

EVIDENCE COLLECTION:

Mark the statement that best describes your desire to pursue a career.

Husband Wife

☐ ☐ I dream about being as effective as possible in my career.

☐ ☐ I value my family more when they value my career.

☐ ☐ I feel good about my life when I am working hard.

☐ ☐ I like going to work about as much as I like being home.

☐ ☐ I like to go to work but I could give it up.

☐ ☐ I like my time at home better than my time at work.

☐ ☐ I like life best when I don't have to work.

☐ ☐ I gain much more satisfaction from volunteer activities than I do from work.

Look at the two bar graphs below. Picture them as you would the bars on your cell phone or the wireless feature of your computer. Color in how many bars you think you like to operate at in your career. What is your intensity level?

My Career Intensity (Husband)   My Career Intensity (Wife)

Balance Your Enterprises by Efficiency

It is likely that one of you has a higher earning potential than the other. One of you can make more money than the other in the same amount of time. It only makes sense, then, that you put more focus on that spouse's career. It's amazing, however, how often this becomes a point of tension. Fear sets in and makes the entire system harder to operate. You may feel inferior to your spouse, so you demand that you get the same opportunity to build your career. Your spouse must then make sacrifices to enable your pursuit. The end result is less money for the same time investment.

Or you may just be proud. This often happens when the wife has a larger earning capacity than the husband. The male ego goes active and fear takes over. You feel that you are somehow inferior because your wife makes more money than you do. You are afraid that you will lose your hero status with her if she brings home a larger pay-check.  You're aware, however, that she really can make more money than you, so it will take an enormous amount of effort for you to match her potential. If you cannot subdue your pride, you will stubbornly argue for your right to work as hard as necessary.

It does not have to be this way! God created each of you with a specific earning power, so you can balance your career commitments based on your potential rather than your gender.

EVIDENCE COLLECTION:

Mark the statement that best describes you as a couple:

☐ In our marriage, the husband has a much greater earning potential than the wife.

☐ In our marriage, the wife has a much greater earning potential than the husband.

☐ In our marriage, the husband has a moderately greater earning potential than the wife.

☐ In our marriage, the wife has a moderately greater earning potential than the husband.

☐ In our marriage, the husband has a slightly greater earning potential than the wife.

☐ In our marriage, the wife has a slightly greater earning potential than the husband.

☐ In our marriage, we have about the same earning potential.

Now discuss how you feel about the boxes you each checked. Is there a step you can take to improve your earning potential to a level you each feel comfortable with and still protect your relationship? Maybe this next segment will also shed light on the impasse you might still feel.

Balance Your Careers by Cooperation

As your family grows, the demands upon you change. Before you have children, you are free to pursue your careers with whatever commitment you want to make. You can leave home without reservation and stay away as long as necessary since there are no kids at home that need care. When toddlers are in the house, your life changes drastically. Their needs are constant, and you must be attentive around the clock. When your kids enter school, you will feel as if you have gained part of your life back as you regain freedom with some of your daytime hours. During the teen years you will become a spectator to your kids' growth and accomplishments. But teens take a lot of time, especially before they drive, so at least one parent needs to be more focused on your teens' needs. Finally, as your kids leave home to establish their own lives, you will ask yourself the most significant question of your life as you enter your most productive years: "Given that I have more time, how will I use it?"

In each of these stages of your marriage, you will have varying degrees of freedom and energy. Depending on what decisions you make, one or the other of you will be able to put more effort into your career while the other focuses on the needs of your family. If you are going to maximize your career potential, you will most likely need to take turns developing your careers as you balance work with family.

This has certainly been the path we have traveled. Early in our marriage, we decided that I (Bill) would focus intensely on finishing my college degree and establishing myself as a pastor. This worked well when our kids were young because I was making progress in my ability to provide and Pam was able to have the joy of pregnancy and nursing without the rigors of a time clock. She was great at staying on top of our kids' needs during those very important developmental days.

As our children transitioned into school, Pam focused on getting her career developed. She returned to college to finish her degree. She taught more Bible studies for women. She began writing in earnest, first for a newspaper, then for magazines before she secured her first two book contracts. During this period, I flexed more with my schedule and spent more time with our kids so Pam could fit her commitments into her schedule.

> In each of the stages of your marriage, you will have varying degrees of freedom and energy.

As our kids entered their teen years, our dedication to our careers paralleled each other. Our boys were busy with their commitments and needed us differently than they had before. Prior to their teens, they needed nearly constant attention. Now they needed us to be alert to the key moments in their lives. They would move along without incident for a while, and then a big moment would take place. They would experience some success that we needed to applaud or they would make a mistake that needed to be corrected. We had to organize our lives so we would recognize these moments and be able to respond to them. We also delegated certain needs of each child to our individual plates so that we shared the parenting duties and responsibilities.

The whole process reminds us of the way "Tammy" works. Tammy is the affectionate name we have given Pam's GPS for her car. When we first turned it on, the system allowed us to choose a voice. We chose a female voice and, since it was a TomTom brand, we gave her the name Tammy. Tammy is silent for long periods until she wants us to do something. She then interrupts any conversation at any time to make an announcement. "In two miles, turn right. Up ahead, stay left, then take the motorway." She has her own schedule, her own language, and her own sense of timing. We joke about her, but we have found her to be a fascinating and useful addition to our life.

We are now at a stage where we are both free to pursue our careers in high gear. Our kids are grown and living independent lives. We can once again leave our home without worrying about how long we'll be gone. We can get up early, stay up late, walk to the kitchen without our robes, or take a nap in the middle of the day. As a result, our conversations have changed. We talk more about our legacy and what mark we are going to leave on our world. We reminisce about great times we've had, and we challenge each other to consider just how far our influence can go before we get too old to work. We are inspired and overwhelmed by the reality that we are entering the most productive 20 years of our life. We work hard because "we want to" much more than because "we have to."

EVIDENCE COLLECTION:

Circle the stage of life that best describes your life right now.

Newlyweds

In the first years without children

Parents of infants/toddlers

Parents of school-age children

Parents of teenagers

Stepfamily in the adjustment period (first five years)

Stepfamily with school-age children

Stepfamily with teenagers

Empty nesters

Grandparents with childcare duties

What challenges are a part of this stage?

Who should focus more on their career during this stage?

A Motivational Budget

In addition to creating a plan for developing effective careers, you need a budget that reflects the best of who you are as a couple. Budgeting is a difficult process for most couples because each of you spends money according to your motivational style. Your mission is to design a financial style that coordinates your goals with your motivational styles so you can maximize your financial impact.

The Challenge

You have heard that conflict over money is one of the main reasons couples break up. Money is a challenge for most couples, first of all, because we all spend money according to our motivational styles. Decision-Makers commit money to maintain control of the direction of their lives. Inspirers spend money to bring happiness and memories to others. Peacekeepers restrict money to maintain peace and simplicity in their lives. Policy Holders manage money according to rules that have been established.

> Money is a challenge for most couples because we all spend money according to our motivational styles.

This would work very well if you married someone with the same motivational style that you have. The challenge exists because most people choose a spouse who has a different motivational style than they do. To be sure, we are drawn to those with similar styles as friends, but we are romantically attracted to those who have the style we do not possess. We are all agonizingly aware that we are not complete, so we seek out a partner who can bring to our lives what we cannot bring ourselves.

OUR STYLE

Consider our relationship. My (Bill's) style is a combination of a Peacekeeper and a Policy Holder. The Peacekeeper in me is stronger than the Policy Holder, so my primary approach is to simplify our financial program as much as possible. I love automatic payments because I can set them up once and let them take care of themselves. I like decisions that are discussed ahead of time so there are very few surprises in our financial picture. I prefer us to have one checkbook, one savings account, and one credit card because it is simple. Our life is actually more complicated than this, but it is still my preference.

The Policy Holder in me qualifies me to be the one who oversees the payment of our bills and balances our checkbook. In this role, I want to know every time I sit down to pay bills that there is plenty of money in the account. I am amazed at how upset I get when I discover a check that has been written that I knew nothing about. I recognize that my reaction is not realistic because Pam needs freedom to follow God's lead in her life and to make decisions as a full adult. My intellect, however, is usually not sufficient to erase my emotional reaction. Conversely, I am amazed at how great I feel when I finish paying bills and there is a reserve left in the account. I am equally amazed at how frustrated I am when I cannot pay all the bills that are due because of insufficient cash flow.

I (Pam) am primarily an Inspirer. I live to make others believe they can accomplish their God-given dreams. I speak to groups to help them, I write books to help them, and I spend money to help them. My best days are the ones where I see others laugh and learn as they gain hope for their future. I am amazed at how many risks I am willing to take to make this a reality. I will travel anywhere in the world to speak to people. I will commit to an opportunity if it will help others discover their dreams.

I don't know how it developed in me, but I live by the motto, "We will figure it out." This motto kicks into gear whenever I encounter an opportunity that I believe God placed before me. My reaction sounds something like, "Wow, look at this great thing God is doing, and He chose me to be a part of it. I know it will take faith to accomplish, but that is what the Christian life is all about, for 'without faith it is impossible to please God' (Hebrews 11:6). I'm not sure how, but we will work this out if we just walk in obedience."

Every spiritual gifts test I take rates my primary gifts as: Faith, leadership, shepherding, and teaching with faith far outranking the others. When I see a need, I ask myself, "Can I work a little harder to achieve this goal? Can I trust God a little better and hear His voice a little louder so I can discern the provision plan and path for this need?"

I tend to work from the need and look for a way to fund it, while Bill tends to look at the funds to decide if we need it. I have to compliment Bill as his love for God and God's Word have moved him out of his comfort zone into this faith walk over and over again. Bill has learned to accept that sometimes God leads him to commitments even when he can't see how something is going to work out, and he has decided to trust me to guide us through many of these opportunities.

This is a very exciting way to live and has given Bill and me many great adventures together. We married at 20 because I knew it was the right thing, and I knew somehow God would provide miraculously for two college students headed into full-time ministry...and God provided. In almost 30 years of marriage we have faced the challenges of finishing a master's degree, two college degrees, raising three boys, serving in three different churches, and developing a writing and speaking ministry...and God has provided each and every step of the way.

At times it has created conflict as I have to ask Bill to trust me with a new commitment. At other times, as we step onto a stage in Singapore, Germany, or some other fun place to travel, Bill will whisper to me, "I can't believe God has allowed us to do all this. What a dream!" Our life can either be a dream or a nightmare, largely depending on how I manage this "by faith" DNA of mine.

However, under stress, I gravitate toward the Decision-Maker. I get strong convictions about the direction we need to head, and I am convinced that everyone in my family will see the wisdom of it once it kicks into gear. The decision seems so clear to me that I have trouble having patience with anything that slows the process. As the stress intensifies, I want all of my life to be more efficient, and the only way I can see to get there is to maintain decision-making control. At times, this has been a great asset in our marriage as I have responded quickly to ministry opportunities for the two of us. At other times, it has been a source of conflict as I have made commitments without Bill's prior consent that raised his stress level.

I completely understand why Bill gets stressed, because neither of my two personality combinations loves a budget. I see the value, I acknowledge the need, I have all the best intentions in the world to follow one, but budgets are just not much fun for me. We have found that the best system is somewhere between our preferences. Without my style, our life would be boring. Without Bill's style, we would be broke!

YOUR STYLE

To help you get a snapshot of what your motivational combination looks like, fill in the following chart.

Wife's name:	
In the column on the right, rank your motivational styles. Write down I for the strongest, 2 for the next strongest, and so on.	
Decision-Maker	
Inspirer	
Peacekeeper	
Policy Holder	

Husband's name:	
In the column on the right, rank your motivational styles. Write down 1 for the strongest, 2 for the next strongest, and so on.	
Decision-Maker	
Inspirer	
Peacekeeper	
Policy Holder	

God First

The bottom line of all finances is stewardship. God is the owner of everything, and He is directing everything toward the accomplishment of His will. To this end, He has entrusted each of us with a number of resources. These resources are not actually ours because we must leave them behind when our days on earth are ended. They have, however, been put in our care to administer during our stay on earth. To help us keep a clear focus on the stewardship of finances, we have been instructed to give the first part of our income back to God. Most people view this pragmatically—God must need money so we have to give so He will have something to spend.

Our giving, however, has nothing to do with God's needs. It is all about directing our hearts. Jesus was very clear that our hearts are connected to our money. His primary instruction about money is found in Luke 12:34, "For where your *treasure* is, there your *heart* will be also." Whatever you spend money on, you fall in love with! If you spend money on God first, you will be connected to Him and will be motivated to pursue a vibrant, active relationship with Him.

EVIDENCE COLLECTION:

What amount of your income would you like to give to God?

5 percent

10 percent

25 percent

90 percent and live on 10 percent

Something else

Briefly write down why you would like to give this amount.

Make an appointment with your spouse to discuss your preference and the reasons behind it. Discuss where you'd like to give your donations and why.

When you get on the same page in the area of money and finances, you know you are beginning to unlock the code to each other's hearts. It is common for couples to argue over their finances, so harmony in this area pays big dividends in helping you live above the line of success and security with each other.

UNLOCKING THE CODE:
Dinner and Dialogue for a Heart-to-Heart Connection

Your Golden List

There comes a time when you have to write down your plan and keep track of both income and expenses. The list we suggest includes priority areas for each of the motivational styles. Everyone cooperates with the budget better when a part of it includes the foundational motivation builders in each of your lives. Notice the empty lines. Use these to personalize your expenditures. You might want to make a copy of this sheet to use for your discussion. When you are finished filling in the requested information and discussing your goals together, place this form in your bill file or with your checkbook as a reminder of the agreements you have made.

EVIDENCE COLLECTION:

Our Motivational Budget			
Assign To	Description	Monthly	Yearly
☐H ☐W	Income		
	Husband's Salary		
	Wife's Salary		
	Investment Income (itemize)		
	Other Income (itemize)		
	Total Income:		
☐H ☐W	Giving to God		
☐H ☐W	Fixed Expenses		
	Mortgage (or Rent)		
	Property Insurance		
	Utilities—Gas and Electric		
	Utilities—Water and Trash		
	Utilities—Phone and Cable		
	Home Maintenance and Repair		
	Car Payment		
	Gasoline		
	Car Insurance		

	Car Repair and Maintenance		
	Life Insurance		
	Groceries		
	Toiletries		
	Motivational Priorities		
□H □W	**The Decision-Maker**		
	Investments		
	Risks for our future		
			•
□H □W	**The Inspirer**		
	Entertainment		
	Social Events		
	Vacation		
□H □W	**The Peacekeeper**		
	Savings		
	Emergency Fund		
□H □W	**The Policy Holder**		
	Retirement Funds		
	College Fund (for each child)		

	Total Expenses:		
	Discretionary Income (Income minus Expenses):		

The key to making any budget work is responsibility. As a couple, you must take the responsibility to fill in the list of income and expenses and work through the process of negotiating your commitments so your income is greater than your expenses. Then, you must take personal responsibility for the lists that are assigned to you. Our suggestion for making this plan work is:

Step 1: Fill out the financial worksheet. Take plenty of time to work through both the numbers and which of you is best equipped to handle each aspect of your financial world. It will most likely take more than one meeting to settle all the issues involved, but it will be well worth the investment. Remember that this is much more than math. The decisions you make about your money help you give expression to your dreams, your motivations, and your hopes. If things get tense, take a break and reschedule your meeting. Just keep rescheduling until you have finished.

> The decisions you make about your money help you give expression to your dreams, your motivations, and your hopes.

Step 2: Take personal responsibility for everything assigned to you. Make a copy of your financial worksheet for each of you and empower each other to take responsibility. If you are responsible for getting money in the bank, you must be able to make deposits. If you have responsibility for making payments, you must be able to access an account with checks, debit cards, or credit cards.

Step 3: Meet regularly to coordinate financial activity and make adjustments. You can meet weekly, monthly, or quarterly. The key is to meet consistently and willingly. The goal of this meeting is to share with each other how your part of the plan is working. It is best if you include plenty of affirmation in each other's areas of strengths. Financial discussions tend to get emotional, so you might as well make the emotional energy work for you! At these meetings, feel free to make adjustments to the financial plan as necessary.

Tammy, our friendly GPS navigator, is an expert at making adjustments. She is often heard to said, "After the next turn, go straight on!" It is a silly reminder to us that life is filled with unexpected turns, but after each turn we can get back on track and pursue our goals with enthusiasm. After the next turn in your life, go straight on toward your goals!

■ ■ ■

We surveyed couples in our audiences on what was the most romantic gift they have ever been given. There were a few luxurious gifts—a home designed to detail, cars, furs, cruises—but more than anything else were stories such as these:

- We were broke, so my husband drew a rose, and I now carry it in my Bible as a bookmark.

- We couldn't afford Valentine gifts, so my husband wrote me a song.

- We were struggling students, and my wife sold her bike to pay my school bill.

- We couldn't afford Christmas, so we gave each other 25 compliments of Christmas, one per day.

A man said his credit card was stolen, but he decided not to report it because the thief was spending less than his wife did.

Signs That You Are Really Broke:

- American Express calls and says: "Leave home without it!"
- Your idea of a seven-course meal is taking a deep breath outside a fine restaurant.
- You're formulating a plan to rob the food bank.
- You receive care packages from Africa.
- You rob Peter…and then rob Paul.
- You finally clean your house and your car hoping to find change.
- You give blood everyday—for the orange juice.
- McDonald's supplies you with all your kitchen condiments.
- Consumer Credit Counseling services said, "We give up!"[22]
- You and your girlfriend got married for the rice.
- At Christmas, all you could exchange were glances.
- Someone saw you kicking a can down the street, and when asked what you were doing, you said, "Moving."

Chapter 9

Expressing Yourself

"The fruit of the Spirit is...gentleness..."

Has conversation with your spouse ever sounded to you like this? "I twan su ot eb ni csyn twit heac rothe. I dwoul elik ot kthin ttha I nca ttrus uyo dan eshar eth timportan sthing fo ym elif hwit uyo. I wkno ew ear tno tperfec, tbu I twan rou prelationshi ot kwor. I tdon elik ot tadmi ti tbu ta stime I ma dafrai ot nope pu ot uyo, dan I dwoul elik ot tpu ttha dbehin su, fi epossibl."

You want to understand your wife, but you can't quite seem to figure out where she's heading with the conversation. You want to connect to your husband's life, but you sense that he is giving you only part of the story. You have the desire to open up and truly connect with each other, but you are finding it harder to do than you thought it would be. You were hoping that the two of you were natural soul mates and that you would instinctively stay in love forever.

> You were hoping that the two of you were natural soul mates and that you would instinctively stay in love forever.

You really want your relationship to flourish, but you realize pretty quickly that you did not come into this relationship with the right code to decipher what your partner is trying to say to you. If you can find the code, you can create an environment that simplifies your relationship. If you cannot find the code, almost any conversation can leave you confused.

It Is an Enigma

During World War II the Nazis used what were called Enigma machines to encrypt and decipher secret messages. Fortunately, Allied cryptographers were able to analyze and decipher a vast number of these messages.

Wouldn't it be handy to have an Enigma machine to decode your mate's moods, thoughts, and actions? It would be especially handy because the Enigma codes changed daily—just like our mate seems to change!

In the encoded message at the opening of this chapter, you don't need an Enigma machine if you know the code. The message above was formed by simply moving the last letter of each word to the front of the word. Once you decode the message, you discover that your spouse was trying to say to you, "I want us to be in sync with each other. I would like to think that I can trust you and share the important things of my life with you. I know we are not perfect, but I want our relationship to work. I don't like to admit it but at times I am afraid to open up to you, and I would like to put that behind us, if possible."

You can probably respond to messages such as these, but the language of the heart has its own code. Misunderstandings are common in marriage, and getting verbally out of sync with your spouse is an all too common struggle. A husband and wife who want to be good to each other often find themselves hurt by one another and arguing more often than they ever intended.

Sometimes it may feel like a battleground in your home, but it doesn't have to be that way. As you unlock the codes to each other's hearts, you can create a DMZ for your love. Unlocking the codes will be better than the treaty at Versailles or Appomattox. Unlocking the codes to each other's hearts is like unilateral disarmament in a world with no nuclear strongholds, no secret weapons of mass marital destruction. In marriage it is possible to hold peace talks and actually come to an

Your mission is to create a safe house for your relationship.

agreement and live in harmony. Think of this chapter as your own personal secretary of state. It will help you negotiate in a way that you will both win at love.

Your mission is to create a safe house for your relationship. Each of you is a complex collection of thoughts, emotions, training, and life experience. As a result, you respond to each other with both exhilaration and hesitation. When the environment of your

> Your body language says more to your spouse than the words you say and the way you say them.

relationship feels safe, you open up and become more vulnerable. When the environment feels tense or perilous, you pull back or create conflict. The goal is to maintain a consistent environment of encouragement and vulnerability where security and success can flourish.

Your Safe House's Bodyguard

Communication tends to be more vulnerable and satisfying when your home feels like a safe house. In law enforcement, a safe house is a secret place that secures a witness from all harm so they can stay alive and testify. In creating a relational safe house, the first and most important element is to create a gentle atmosphere.

The bodyguard that will help you develop a safe environment in your relationship is your body language. Your body speaks volumes to your spouse. In fact, your body language says more to your spouse than the words you say and the way you say them. If they are paying attention, others can tell a lot about you by noticing your body language:

- They can tell if you are angry.
- They can predict the emotions in your heart.
- They can tell if you are trying to intimidate them.
- They can discern your attitude.
- They can tell when your attitude has improved.
- They can tell when you are sad.

- They can tell when you have had a significant spiritual experience.
- They can tell you are sincere.
- They can tell if you respect them.
- They can tell when your heart is filled with joy.
- They can tell if there is romantic attraction.

Let Your Body Talk

Most of us are accidental in our body language. We simply do what we do without thinking about the message we are conveying. When you consider that more than 50 percent of the message you communicate to your spouse is based on your body language, it makes sense to think through what your body is saying. Here are a few simple truths about body language to keep in mind.

The smaller your audience, the smaller your body motions should be.

If you are speaking to a group, you'll want to use bigger hand motions, stand on your feet, and cover enough space on the stage to engage the crowd. If you are engaged in a private conversation, you'll want to keep your hands closer to your body and use smaller motions as you communicate. Large motions in close proximity give one of two messages. You are either insecure and are trying to make sure the other person doesn't get too close or you are trying to intimidate the other person to gain an advantage.

You project interest when you lean toward another person.

If you want your spouse to know you are interested in what is being shared, gently lean forward. The same is true if you face your partner, so the communication is more eye to eye. Turning your back, walking away, or looking elsewhere when communicating to your mate sends the clear signal, "I am busy with things more important than you right now." However, when you put down what is in your hands, look away from the computer screen toward your mate, turn your chair, this says to your spouse, "I am listening, I want to hear what you have to say, and it is safe to share. I will gently accept what you say and guard your heart in the process."

You give a message of safety when you open up your posture.

If you are sitting with your arms and your legs crossed, you make it clear that you are not really open to a conversation. Your spouse will sense that you would rather be with someone else. If your hands are resting on your legs and both your legs are parallel to the floor, your spouse will instantly sense that you are interested in the conversation at hand. Even better, reaching out for your spouse communicates in a powerful way, "I value you and what you are about to say."

Gentle physical contact is a powerful safety net.

You can quickly encourage your spouse through a gentle touch or hug. Our bodies are wired to release endorphins when we are affectionate with another human being. The result is a lower heart rate, lower blood pressure, relaxed muscles, and a general sense of well-being. This is why we often recoil from our spouses when we are not ready to be touched. It isn't that we don't want to be touched. It's just that it has such a powerful impact on us.

Eye contact makes all the difference.

You look at people you are interested in. Your eyes, more than any other part of your body, express what is really going on in your heart. When you are ashamed, you avoid eye contact. When you are embarrassed, you avoid eye contact. When you are upset, you avoid eye contact. On the other hand, you will make eye contact when there is trust, appreciation, or fascination.

You need to be a little careful because if you just stare at your spouse, you will create an uncomfortable feeling. You stare at people if you are interrogating them, and you stare at people if you lack social skills. The key is to make consistent eye contact. You will want to look away every few seconds and then reengage eye contact. You also want to concentrate on relaxing the muscles around your eyes. If you tense your eye muscles, your forehead will wrinkle and you will give the impression that you disagree with what is being said.

Give the gift of a pleasant look when communicating with your spouse. Even if you are upset, you don't have to throw daggers with your eyes. Decide to wear the expression, "I am giving you the benefit of the doubt."

Most of us instinctively know these things if we were raised in a healthy, safe home. If we were not raised in that kind of environment, we will need to consciously work on improving our body language to help open up our mate (and engage in conversation with those we love). Even those who were raised in an emotionally healthy environment can get self-absorbed, stressed, or lazy and just slack off using the body language that says, "You are valuable. You are worth my time and energy." Body language can say all that before a word is ever spoken.

> **Decoder Moment:** Stop right now, when you are not upset, and decide the best "body language" way to sit or stand when talking with your spouse. Try different poses, like a model, and ask for feedback from your mate to learn his or her favorite one.

The Tone of Your Safe House

In addition to having a bodyguard posted at your relational safe house, you will want to focus on the tone of your conversations. Many homes today have an alarm system to protect them from intrusion and to alert the residents of the presence of smoke and carbon monoxide. When everything is okay, the system emits a variety of beeps and signals. These are the sounds that say, "Everything is okay. It's all right to roam freely around the house." When something is wrong in the house, the system lets out a shrill sound that disturbs everyone in the house.

Your relationship has an alarm system that either announces that all is okay or disturbs everyone in the home. To turn the system on or off, you will also likely need an alarm code. In relationships, the alarm system that indicates that all is well is your tone of voice. While body language is by far the most important ingredient in your communication, the tone of your voice is not far behind in the influence it has on the climate of your relationship.[23] A gentle tone of voice will raise the safety level of your love and minimize conflict. A harsh tone will create distance between you and your partner.

> A gentle tone of voice will raise the safety level of your love and minimize conflict.

> A gentle answer turns away wrath,
>> but a harsh word stirs up anger.
>> (Proverbs 15:1)

People do not think much about their tone of voice as they are growing up. From your earliest days, you have reacted to the people you grew up around. They made you happy and you responded. They seemed unreasonable and you resisted. They were irritating and you reacted. Since these people were around during your most formative years, they had a profound impact on who you are today. It is possible that your skill in choosing your tone of voice from conversation to conversation developed well, but it is more likely that you simply reacted to what happened around you.

The tone in your voice will give people one of two impressions about you. Some tones will cause people to believe that you are gentle toward them. Your voice will reassure them that you care about them and that you are safe to talk with. Other tones give people the impression you are trying to gain control over them. Your voice will challenge them and persuade them that you are trying to get the upper hand in the conversation. Your agenda may not be clear to them, but they get the distinct impression that you do have an agenda that does not have their best interests in mind.

A tone of voice that tells people you are gentle will be characterized by:

- *Softness.* A soft voice calms everyone down.

- *Drop in inflection.* The inflection in your voice will go down a little at the end of your sentences. The trailing off of your voice expresses sincerity, making you more believable.

- *Appropriateness.* The tone in your voice is appropriate for the conversation. Life is lived out in a variety of situations and surprises to which we must all react. If your spouse just received a promotion at work and you react with an affirming tone of voice, your partner will be encouraged. If there is a kitchen fire and you scream at your mate to help, he or she will respond by jumping in.

A tone of voice that tells people you are trying to gain control over them will be characterized by:

- *Loudness.* A loud voice will put people on the alert and cause them to take a defensive posture with you—unless you are carrying a message of thrill, excitement, or good news. People can handle a little more volume when the messenger is carrying positive news.

- *Harshness.* When there is a bite in your voice, the person you are talking with will become defensive. The introverts will shut down while the extroverts will argue with you.

- *Rise in inflection.* The inflection of your voice will rise at the end of a sentence. Other people will think you are selling something or tying to convince them of something.

- *Inappropriateness.* Your inflection is not appropriate to the situation. If your wife announces that she got a promotion at work and you get angry, she will be confused. If there is a kitchen fire and your husband calmly approaches you and softly says, "The stove is on fire," you will wonder what in the world is wrong with him!

- *Other negative gestures.* A negative tone is sometimes carried by short, choppy sentences or accompanied with sighs of exasperation, frustration, or rolling of the eyes. Sometimes it is easier to catch yourself doing these actions even if you can't hear when your tone of voice changes from positive to negative. If you can't hear the difference, you can decide to quit flailing your arms, stomping your feet, rolling your eyes, or huffing in exasperation. If you curb those, chances are you will also curb your tone of voice. (Clue: If you were to write what you are saying and you used all CAPS, the tone would probably be negative if you said it aloud.)

You are generally the last one to be aware of your tone of voice. You are so attached to your life and your reactions to it that your senses grow dull when it comes to recognizing the influence of your voice. You can sharpen your senses by deliberately listening to yourself and asking, "How would I respond if my spouse or a good friend used the tone of voice I just used?"

You can also ask someone you trust to evaluate your tone of voice for you. This could be your spouse, a friend, or a trusted colleague at work. This works only if you give this person explicit permission to evaluate you. You can say something like, "For the next week, will you point out to me when I do well with my tone of voice and when I push people away with my tone?" Give a time limit so this does not become the definition of your relationship and decide ahead of time that you will take what they say seriously. If not, you will grow defensive rather than grow through their insight.

> You are generally the last one to be aware of your tone of voice.

Decoder Moment: Pretend to be upset at your mate. First use an exasperated, frustrated tone of voice and say, "I have something I need to talk to you about."

Next use a compassionate, empathetic tone and say, "I have something I need to talk to you about."

Can you hear the difference?

(If you are brave, ask your spouse to do an imitation of you when you are mad at them and see how you like it when your mate talks to you how you talk to them. Bill did this for me one day and said, "How would you like it if I answered you like this?" Then he mimicked me word for word, tone for tone. I answered him, "That was too good. I hate it. Sorry. I will try harder." I still have to try hard to monitor my tone when I'm under a lot of stress. I can easily revert to old habits, but knowing it is a slippery slope for me helps me be more aware and make better choices most of the time.)

Decorating Your Safe House

It is a remarkable finding that words are a relatively small part of intimate communication. Emotions are primarily communicated through body language and tone of voice so the actual words can be overrun by the nonverbals. Don't let that fool you, though. Your words may be small, but they are very important to the quality of your communication. And men and women approach the use of words very differently:

> A husband read an article to his wife about how many words women use a day: 30,000 to a man's 15,000. The wife replied, "The reason has to be because we have to repeat everything to men." The husband turned to his wife and asked, "What?"

Words are vital, and we need to use them. Every word you use either adds to the safety level of your love or threatens your ability to build a secure, growing relationship. Just as with the rest of communication, there are words that confirm a gentle environment where it is safe to be vulnerable and there are words that cause your spouse to believe you are trying to gain control.

Words that RAISE the safety net on your relationship and create a gentle approach to your spouse include:

Respect. Statements of honor and respect. You can say, "I am proud of you," or "You are remarkable at _____ (fill in the blank)," at any time, regardless of how you feel at the moment. The best traits of your spouse do not change with the current emotional climate of your relationship.

Affirmation. Simple statements such as, "You are safe with me," "I will guard whatever you share with me," "You have time to grow in my book," "We don't need to be perfect. Let's just work on being a little better by this time next year," give your spouse permission to share with you. It is important that you say these things only if you commit to follow through with them. A promise to protect the confidentiality of your spouse is a very valuable gift. If you then tell other people what you promised to protect, the hurt will be multiplied.

> Words are vital, and we need to use them. Every word you use either adds to the safety level of your love or threatens your ability to build a secure, growing relationship.

"I" statements. Most conversations go better when you speak about your needs and the way life is affecting you. The tendency is to point out what you don't like in your spouse, which breeds defensiveness. "For some reason, it is very upsetting to me when we arrive late," is much different than "You make me so mad because you are always late." Both statements make it clear that you would like to see something change. The first statement allows your spouse to safely enter the conversation. The second statement forces your spouse to put up defenses.

Sincerity. We are told in the Bible to "speak the truth in love" (Ephesians 4:15). This means that you get to say some really nice things to your spouse, and it means you will have to share some tough things with your spouse. In either case, you can usually navigate the conversations if you are seeking your spouse's best interests. We all have a tendency to play games in communication to either gain our spouse's attention or just to smooth things over. Either of these approaches eventually gives the impression that you have an agenda and are seeking control rather than sincerely loving your mate.

Encouragement. Give sincere compliments; look for ways to build up your mate. "Encourage one another and build each other up" is a command given to us by God (1 Thessalonians 5:11). It is a picture of building a solid home and sheltering it with a reliable roof. On our honeymoon, Bill told me, "Pam, I will be your mirror." That simple statement, whispered to me as he held my face in his hands, has become a sturdy shelter for our love.

You'll Pay for That!

Words that are negative proclaim the message that you trying to gain control over your spouse. It is common to fall into the use of negative words:

> A couple drove down a country road for several miles, not saying a word. An earlier discussion had led to an argument, and neither of them wanted to concede their position. As they passed a barnyard of mules, goats, and pigs, the husband asked sarcastically, "Relatives of yours?"
>
> "Yep," the wife replied. "In-laws."

An easy way to remember what *not* to say is to remind yourself that if you use these words, you will be in a whole lot of PAIN:

Past. Reminders of past failures and mistakes rob from the relationship and are often used as weapons to gain the emotional upper hand. To be sure, we all make mistakes and steps must be taken to insure those mistakes do not happen again. It does no good, however, to bring up the mistakes of the past over and over again. Eventually, your spouse will conclude that you don't care about the relationship, you care only about winning.

> It does no good to bring up the mistakes of the past over and over again.

Accusations. When the environment in your home gets testy, it is common to judge the intentions of your spouse's heart by using a lot of "you" statements. If you get in the habit of consistently pointing to your spouse's behavior as the problem in your relationship, you will make it unsafe for your spouse to open up to you. If you act as if you know what's going on inside and you make value judgments based on your conclusions instead of what your spouse tells you, you undermine the relationship.

Insults and name calling. Your spouse can push triggers in your life that nobody else even knows exist. This can be irritating and unnerving. God allows these triggers to be pushed because He wants to help you heal in those areas so they don't have so much control in your life. This is easy to say when you are calm and relaxed, but it is tough to remember when your emotions are in a frenzy. This is generally when the insults and name calling are at their worst.

The degrading way that some partners talk to each other is a truly amazing thing to us. You cannot possibly create a safe environment if you are swearing at each other or calling each other horrible names. If this is a struggle for you, talk with a counselor or pastor or trusted spiritual leader as soon as possible. Ask for help in figuring out why you are so harsh to the person you promised to love for the rest of your life.

> Your spouse can push triggers in your life that nobody else even knows exist.

Neglect. The ultimate betrayal is to refuse to communicate, refuse to have sex, refuse to interact in handling life's responsibilities. It is the equivalent of saying, "I quit. I don't value you. I don't value us. I don't value our life or our love. I am done here." Giving the cold shoulder might make you feel as if you have the power in the relationship, but all you are really doing is slowly unraveling your love. Just as you might unravel an afghan by tugging at one string, refusing to communicate unravels the relationship because it erodes trust by making the other person feel so devalued that they are invisible to you.

Gentle Power

The goal of your safe house is to create a gentle environment in your conversations with one another. Gentleness is another powerful force in loving relationships. Many people resist the idea of gentleness because it doesn't seem strong and it feels like a vulnerable position to be in. Just the opposite is true. Gentleness is the realization that love can flourish only where there is grace.

You are alive because God gave you life despite the mistakes you've made along the way. You have salvation because God gave His Son to pay the price for the punishment you deserved. You have opportunities because His grace transformed you from a lost individual to "God's workmanship, created in Christ Jesus to do good works, which God prepared in advance for us to do" (Ephesians 2:10).

> Gentleness is the realization that love can flourish only where there is grace.

Gentleness has produced some of the most important results in life.

Gentleness makes people great and prepares them for the battles of life. In Psalm 18:34-36, David reviews the secret to his ability as a soldier:

> He trains my hands for battle;
> my arms can bend a bow of bronze.
> You give me your shield of victory,
> and your right hand sustains me;
> you stoop down to make me great.
> You broaden the path beneath me,
> so that my ankles do not turn.

He realized that the gentleness of God created in him a strength that he could never have discovered on his own.

Eventually, gentle people will be in charge. "Blessed are the gentle, for they shall inherit the earth" (Matthew 5:5 NASB). Gentle people build strong networks and develop trust with people. There may be situations where controlling people run the show, but in the end, the gentle will be given the positions of trust.

Gentleness keeps us honest about ourselves. Sometimes we have to challenge each other because we are all imperfect. We need others who will coach us through situations and point out areas that need growth. If you offer your evaluation in order to control the behavior of others, you will come across as judgmental. If you offer your insight with gentleness, however, you will guard your heart from temptation and promote growth for everyone involved. "Brothers, if someone is caught in a sin, you who are spiritual should restore him gently. But watch yourself, or you also may be tempted" (Galatians 6:1).

Gentleness demonstrates your respect for God's presence. "Let your gentleness be evident to all. The Lord is near" (Philippians 4:5). If you believe God is near and is in control of life, you will treat people with gentleness because you will realize they need the same grace as you. You will trust that God will direct your life and the lives of others to accomplish His will.

Gentleness produces wisdom. "Who among you is wise and understanding? Let him show by his good behavior his deeds in the gentleness of wisdom" (James 3:13 NASB). "But the wisdom from above is first pure, then peaceable, gentle, reasonable, full of mercy and good fruits, unwavering, without hypocrisy" (James 3:17 NASB). When God gives wisdom to people, it is characterized by gentleness. This wisdom endures all the challenges of life and promotes outstanding relationships.

Gentleness empowers you to stand up. "But in your hearts set apart Christ as Lord. Always be prepared to give an answer to everyone who asks you to give the reason for the hope that you have. But do this with gentleness and respect" (1 Peter 3:15). Gentleness gives you a secure place to operate from so that you are more sure of who you are and what you believe. When you talk about what is important to you, it comes across as sure and stable because you don't need others to agree with you to convince you that what you believe is true. In marriage, this makes you a partner who can give rather than take. You can share your opinions, encourage your spouse, and accept imperfections because you don't need your partner to be exactly like you.

> When God gives wisdom to people, it is characterized by gentleness.

The Fear of Control

The challenge to communication in marriage is wrapped around your vulnerability to your spouse. Intimacy opens a tunnel in your heart that allows your mate to have great influence over your emotions, your confidence, and your ability to trust. If there is a strong safety net, trust is high and vulnerability is a welcome state in life. If the safety net is tentative, trust is low and each partner will take a defensive stand against the other.

This is a common fear for human beings because we are all inherently self-centered. It didn't take long in life to learn the word *mine*. On the honorable side, we believe that our perspective in life is the correct perspective. We, therefore, argue for our perspective and convince others that they would be better off if they agree with us.

> The challenge to communication in marriage is wrapped around your vulnerability to your spouse.

On the darker side, we want to control the behavior of others in order to feel better about ourselves. We mistakenly believe that our lives will be improved by the way other people act. This creates an endless circle of insecurity. We tell others what to do out of insecurity. They do what we told them. We conclude they do not have enough strength to decide for themselves and are dependent upon us. Their weakness means we cannot really trust them, which makes us more insecure. Therefore, we tell them to change so that we can be more secure, and the cycle begins again.

Active or Passive?

You may have chosen passive skills that help you maintain control of your environment. You make verbal commitments that you never follow through on. You delay discussions until it's too late to do anything about the issue at hand. You make safe commitments with your time that enable you to operate far below your potential. You take on leadership positions but slow down every decision with long discussions and overly careful examination. You say you will handle certain responsibilities, and then you just never get around to doing it. You don't tell your spouse no or pass it back, you just drop the ball.

Passive-aggressive behavior can be an aggravating trait:

> A husband and wife were involved in a petty argument, both
> of them unwilling to admit they might be in error.
>
> "I'll admit I'm wrong," the wife told her husband in a concil-
> iatory attempt, "if you'll also admit I'm right."
>
> He agreed and, like a gentleman, insisted she go first.
>
> "I'm wrong," she said.
>
> With a twinkle in his eye, he responded, "You're right!"

You may have aggressive skills that help you hold on to control. You argue with anyone who disagrees with you. You make demands of your spouse and kids in the morning and keep them going throughout the day so that no one else can infringe upon your agenda. You become argumentative when your loved ones get too close. You refuse to ever say, "I'm sorry," and you have an explanation for everything you do that focuses on the intention of your heart rather than your behavior. At the same time, you are critical of other people's behavior and dismiss the value of their intentions.

The end result is that nobody can get close enough to you to ever change your agenda and no one can get close enough to you to ever make you feel better about yourself. You feel safe but you feel alone.

Feeling Numb

This has been a significant issue for both of us. As I (Bill) discussed previously, my mom is a highly creative woman with a strong personality. At the same time, she was scared of many things in life because of some traumatic experiences during her teen years. Her response was to use her strength to control everything in her life, including her husband and kids. I now know she just wanted to feel safe, but I could not figure that out during my teen years.

My first reaction was to become numb. I had witnessed my older sister and brother argue with her, but I concluded they lost every interaction so I went the other direction. I shut down much of my emotional reaction to life so that I couldn't be hurt. You could yell at me and I would feel nothing. You could criticize me and I would feel nothing.

You could challenge me and I would feel nothing. This worked well for me until I was sixteen years old and met Jesus as my Savior.

He was not content to let me be numb. The more I grew in my relationship with Jesus, the more my emotional life awakened. I started feeling things in my heart, which I loved even though they made me uncomfortable. I began to care about people in a way I never even imagined existed. I had learned to not trust people, so I stayed aloof from everyone. I had very few memorable moments with friends because the only things I did other than school were with the members of my immediate family. All of a sudden, I was meeting other people who knew Jesus, and deep friendships were developing with little effort.

At the same time, I began to get irritated with things in life. Prior to this, I was never upset with my parents because I was numb. It didn't really matter what they did because I could disappear into my shell and keep myself busy. I didn't have quarrels with people at school because I didn't feel anything. I didn't have any significant friendships so I didn't have any significant disagreements. I was now introduced to the world of conflict. I grew irritated with my mom's controlling behavior and my dad's refusal to intervene. In my junior year of high school, I developed a couple of contentious acquaintances. I was involved in sports with these young men so I couldn't avoid them. I didn't want to back off, but I also didn't know what to do because I didn't have experience in handling conflict. As a result, I would absorb the criticism without saying anything, and I would become more determined to succeed in the face of the quarrel.

It was overwhelming going from very few emotions to interacting with the sensations of life. Although I was growing, I replaced my numbness with an uncomfortable undercurrent of irritation. I was learning how to move forward despite my mom's controlling behavior, but I didn't want other controlling relationships in my life. My experience at being numb easily translated into passive skills to maintain my sense of control. I made commitments that were smaller than my abilities. I kept a controlled schedule, even though I was capable of a faster pace. I avoided situations that I could not lead. I figured if I was in charge, I would have control.

Meeting Pam convinced me that I was missing out on a lot of life by thinking I had to be in control of everything. She was talented in areas I only dreamed of. She was bolder than I was and was willing to make big commitments to force growth in her life. I found these incredibly attractive and believed I could benefit greatly by learning from her how to do that.

It still makes me nervous at times because she makes commitments that make me feel out of control. She has such a long track record now of success in these commitments that I have learned to trust the way God moves in her life despite how I may feel when I first hear about what we are going to do next.

The Rescuer

My (Pam's) experience growing up was the opposite of Bill's. His mom tried to control everything while my dad was out of control. My dad's alcoholic rages would dominate our social life (friends and family would scatter when he became volatile), and his moods controlled our literal safety. (We'd push furniture against the door so he couldn't come into our room.)

My role in our family was to be the one who "stood down" my father and told him his behaviors were inappropriate. Or I would usher my younger siblings outside to Grandma's or to a friend's so Dad couldn't get to us.

When life feels out of control, that instinctive urge of self-preservation kicks in, and it often isn't pretty. If I do not feel safe, I can get a "battle sergeant" persona going as I feel the need to fight for my rights, my plan, my way, my environment to return to a safe one.

Fortunately, Bill is a gentle man so this ugly side of Pam, the General Patton Pam, rarely is seen. But it isn't just Bill's gentleness that works to tame the savage beast in me; God's calming Spirit has trained me to believe verses such as, "Whoever wants to become great among you must be your servant, and whoever wants to be first must be slave of all" (Mark 10:43-44).

My choice to react as a servant diffuses the tension because my trust isn't just in Bill's gentleness but in God's. As I seek to be more like Jesus, the Lamb of God who sacrificed His life out of love, I gain the ability to serve rather than fight. I can trust that God's gentle plan is better than my military operations.

UNLOCKING THE CODE:
Dinner and Dialogue for a Heart-to-Heart Connection

Practice Your Expressions

There are a number of possible ways to create a gentle, safe environment in your love relationship:

1. Practice body language that conveys the message, "You are safe with me." You can practice this on your own or you can work on it as a couple. The key is to create practice sessions where you do not evaluate yourself too hard. You just practice. As with any skill, it starts out very awkward, but the more you practice, the more natural it becomes. Practice expressing the following emotions without using words:

   • Happiness

   • Joy

   • Enthusiasm

   • Affection

   • Agreement

   • Determination

   • Frustration

   • Disgust

   • Confusion

- Disagreement
- Disappointment

A fun way to practice these in a less threatening way is in a game of charades. Each of you select half the list and take turns acting out those emotions.

2. Practice choosing your tone of voice. Just like body language, you can practice on your own or together as a couple. The key is to train your ears to hear your own tone of voice. If you are practicing on your own, you may even want to record yourself saying phrases you would like to share with your spouse. As you play it back to yourself, you will gain a new perspective on how you sound to your mate. Use the same list above and see if you can express these emotions with your tone of voice. Use the same sentence, "Life is a great journey." Repeat it for each emotion and see if you can convey it with the tone in your voice.

3. Set a weekly time to talk with your spouse. It is helpful if you choose questions ahead of time to discuss so you avoid talking about responsibilities, bills, and challenges. It is easier to connect on an intimate level if you are talking about hopes, dreams, and personal growth, but these seldom happen by accident. Consider the following questions as a starting point:

- How have your dreams in life changed over the past five years?
- What has been your favorite adventure during the past year?
- If you could travel to anyplace in the world, where would you want to go and why?
- If you described your life right now as a sporting event, what event would it be? Why?

- If you described your life right now as a song, what title would that song have? Why?

- If you could spend an entire day with anyone in the world, who would you want to spend the day with? What would you want to ask that person?

4. Give your spouse permission to talk to you about any topic. Decide you will simply listen and withhold your opinion unless you are asked to give it.

5. Create an introduction that alerts your spouse to your need to have a safe environment for an upcoming conversation. Phrases such as, "I want to talk with you, but I am a little nervous," "I need you to be gentle with me right now," "Can we take some time to dialogue?" are all straightforward ways to alert your spouse that your need for safety is high. If you have trouble establishing this, it might be good to attend a Marriage Encounter weekend to learn the process of dialoguing that includes writing out what you would like to share first and then reading your letters to each other.

6. As a couple, create a fun way to express your need for a safe place. You might have a box of Band-aids that you can set on his or her desk, a white flag you can wave, or even an umbrella you can pop open as your way of saying, "Can we move out of the storm?" This tangible symbol can help you two when you have one of those prolonged, "things have escalated out of control" arguments, and you both know you need a new way to begin again.

Choose the steps you believe will create the most safety. Connecting to your spouse is tricky business. Few experiences in life are more satisfying than the moments you are connected spiritually, emotionally, and physically. If you have not tasted it together, you will sense a nagging desire in your heart to have more in your relationship. Once you have tasted the benefits of true connection, you will desire it for the rest of your life.

Arm your relationship today with a safe environment that will maximize your growth and create a true partnership in your journey. Your relationship can be your safe house on earth.

> Once you have tasted the benefits of true connection, you will desire it for the rest of your life.

■ ■ ■

Never try to guess your wife's size. Just buy her anything marked "petite" and hold on to the receipt.

> How to answer the world's hardest question for a husband: "Do I look fat in this?"
>
> Husband's safe reply: "I can't tell. I'm so bedazzled by your beauty I can't think straight."

ABOVE THE LINE
_____
BELOW THE LINE

A man and his wife were having some problems at home and were giving each other the silent treatment. Suddenly, the man realized that the next day, he would need his wife to wake him at 5:00 a.m. for an early-morning business flight. Not wanting to be the first to break the silence (and lose), he wrote on a piece of paper, "Please wake me at 5:00 a.m." He left it where he knew she would find it.

The next morning, he woke up, only to discover it was 9:00 a.m. and he had missed his flight. Furious, he was about to go and see why his wife hadn't wakened him, when he noticed a piece of paper by the bed. On the paper was written, "It is 5:00 a.m. Wake up."[24]

Chapter 10

Accessing the Marriage Code

"The fruit of the Spirit is…self-control."

I (Bill) recently upgraded to a new laptop computer. I was looking for one that had plenty of horsepower and would travel well. I, therefore, wanted a small case but a relatively large screen. I spent hours in a number of stores looking at various models and found one that I thought would meet all my needs. It even had a swivel screen that would turn 360 degrees! I thought, *What a cool age I live in. This is an amazing piece of technology. It works fast, can be a lot fun, and looks good too!*

I didn't discover until I got home a small metal sensor on the side of the screen, and in guy-like fashion, I decided to touch it before I read anything about it. An interesting message appeared, "Access denied. Your fingerprints are not programmed into the system. Would you like to add your information to the system?"

I got all excited. I had a high-tech, crime-fighting fingerprint identification system on my laptop! Of course, I enthusiastically clicked on the button marked "Yes" and entered the process. I had to go through a number of security steps to validate my identity. First, I had to confirm that I had an authentic version of the operating system for my computer. Then I had to enter my username and password to confirm that it was actually me who was setting up my fingerprints. I then had to reenter my password to confirm that I could type the same word two times in a row. Then I had to swipe one of my fingers across the sensor. Apparently, swiping your fingerprint is the same as typing your password because I had to repeat the swipe to prove that I could make the same motion with my hand two times in a row. Having completed that, I had to swipe a different finger twice to finish the process of authenticating that my fingers are attached to my body.

By the time I was done, I felt very important. I now had a new laptop with two different ways to access all the information that is vital to me. I could still enter my username and password or I could swipe my finger across the sensor.

The first time I actually used the fingerprint sensor, I couldn't help but think of all the ways access is restricted to people today. In addition to usernames, passwords, and fingerprint systems, we have account numbers and Personal Identification Numbers. In sophisticated professional settings, we even use retinal scanners and voiceprint sensors to confirm our identities. The bottom line is that you cannot gain access unless you have the access code that will open up the well of information.

Just as the information we consider important is available to all who have the access code, a secure, successful marriage is available to anyone who practices the eight principles discussed in this book.

Mystery of love
Affection
Recreation
Resolving conflicts
Intimacy
Activating the alarms
Golden goals
Expressing yourself

As you can see, the eight skills to a better marriage—one that is "above the line" in success and security—look simple. They can be—if you want to use them! Just as a PIN will give you access to your mate's bank account or a password gives you the ability to read your mate's computer, desire will give you the ability to move your relationship over the line.

In all our years of teaching, equipping, and counseling, the one skill that we have seen as the most vital is the desire to want a marriage that is "above the line." No one can make you want a better marriage; that is a choice only you can make. But we do know an easier way to gain this desire. Ask God. God created marriage, so He has the access codes to both your hearts.

If you are not at a place where you have that desire, you can honestly pray something like, "God, give me the 'want to' to want to make my marriage better. Help me have the desire to desire my mate." Start where you are. One researcher put it like this:

> I think that a lot of what's wrong with relationships is that this information is just not known. Eventually everyone is going to know this stuff. And nobody's going to know where it came from. It's sort of like brushing your teeth or flossing— who thought of flossing? Who thought of this stuff? Nobody remembers who thought of it. It's just a good idea.[25]

Your long-term goal is to develop a level of skill in your life that empowers you to grow in the most important areas of marriage and enables you to invest in a healthy, vibrant relationship. The mission will be strenuous because your heart has the tendency to be distracted, deceived, and destructive to you and the ones you love.

The best way we know of to accomplish this mission is to pursue a personal relationship with Jesus Christ. He died for you because He recognized the fallen condition of your heart. He knew that you could not possibly pay the price yourself for your mistakes, but He knew that He could pay an eternal price that would never run out. He then committed to send the Holy Spirit into the heart of everyone who trusted Him for salvation. The Holy Spirit brings with Him a deep love for your spouse and insight into every one of the codes that will unleash the potential of your marriage.

> The Holy Spirit brings with Him a deep love for your spouse and insight into every one of the codes that will unleash the potential of your marriage.

If this is still something you can't quite get your mind wrapped around, that's all right. We'll try to explain it in several ways with some real-life examples so you can see how it works.

Simply put, the Holy Spirit is God's Spirit. When you make a decision to begin a relationship with God, God sends His Spirit to live in your soul so that He is there to whisper new thoughts, new ways, and new insights that will enhance your life and all your relationships. Since God takes up residence in your heart and mind, you no longer have to muddle through life and the relationship puzzle alone. The God who personally designed each of you is there to give you direction. It's kind of like having the engineer who first drew the plans for your car not just hand you the Owner's Manual but volunteer to be your personal chauffeur.

You Have a Choice

Whoever officiated your wedding probably made a statement similar to, "By the authority vested in me by God, I now pronounce you husband and wife in the name of the Father, the Son, and the Holy Spirit."

Husband and wife.

It seemed like it was going to be so easy. You had a new title, new dreams, and enough love to build a life together. You figured that the usernames of *husband* and *wife* would be enough to access each other's heart and body.

The problem is that we all have a battle going on inside of us. The apostle Paul addressed his good friends in the city of Ephesus about the battle in their hearts. In each and every one of us are two natures that are alive and well. Paul calls them the old self and the new self. The old self is the fallen nature that is corrupted by sin and addicted to the desires of the flesh. The new self is in love with Jesus and longs to follow the leadership of the Holy Spirit. Every moment of our lives, we need to choose sides. You can choose to access the part of your heart that is dominated by the old self and deal with the results or you can access the part of your heart that is ruled by the Holy Spirit and enjoy the benefits. It's your choice.

As you consider the choice of which nature to follow, check out the specification sheet for each of these access points:

The Old Self
(see Ephesians 4 for more information)

Operating System (the main control program of your life): Yourself

Processor: Futile thinking with darkened understanding (vv. 17-18)

Display: Falsehood (v. 25) with lost sensitivity (v. 19)

Memory: Continual lust for more (v. 19)

Graphics Card: Indulged with sensuality and every kind of impurity (v. 19)

Networking: Separated from the life of God (v. 18)

Hard Drive: Deceitful desires (corrupted) (v. 22)

Security Software: Hard-hearted ignorance (v. 18)

Productivity Software: Stealing (v. 28), brawling and slander, every form of malice (v. 31)

I/O Ports: Bitterness, rage, and anger (v. 31)

Speakers: Unwholesome talk (v. 29)

Basic Warranty: Voided (part of your former way of life) (v. 22)

The New Self
(see Ephesians 4 for more information)

Operating System (the main control program of your life): Christ

Processor: The truth that is in Jesus (v. 21)

Display: True righteousness (v. 24)

Memory: The Holy Spirit of God (v. 30)

Graphics Card: Holiness (v. 24)

Networking: Members of one body (v. 25)

Hard Drive: New attitude of your minds (v. 23)

Security Software: Hearing and being taught truth (v. 21)

Productivity Software: Doing something useful with your own hands (v. 28)

I/O Ports: Kindness, compassion, forgiveness (v. 32)

Speakers: Speak truthfully—benefits those who listen (vv. 25,29)

Basic Warranty: Sealed by the Holy Spirit for the day of redemption (v. 30)

The Ultimate Upgrade

It doesn't take long to realize that the new self is far superior to the old self, but you know it is not as simple as intellectually identifying which option is better. Dr. Phil has made the phrase, "So, how is that working for you?" popular because so many couples try to navigate their relationships with the old self. If you've never met Jesus as your personal Savior, you have access only to the old self. You may have worked hard to discipline yourself, but you still have only yourself to work with. More likely, you have worked hard to make your relationship work, but it is just not what you had hoped it would be.

Those who have invited Jesus to live within them and be the boss of their lives have a choice. They can choose to gain access to the old self and live according to their desires. In fact, it's common for believers to do so because the battle is intense, and the old self is constantly begging for attention. They have a different choice, however. They can log in to the new self and draw on the power of the Holy Spirit to love, think, and decide. With this extra resource available to them, they are able to more effectively give of themselves to the pursuits that make for satisfying relationships.

A panel of experts in marriage and family research compiled the following list of the ten most important characteristics in long-term successful marriages:

1. Lifetime commitment to marriage

2. Loyalty to spouse

3. Strong moral values

4. Respect for spouse as a friend

5. Commitment to sexual fidelity

6. Desire to be a good parent

7. Faith in God and spiritual commitment

8. Desire to please and support spouse

9. Good companion to spouse

10. Willingness to forgive and be forgiven[26]

Each of these traits is best accomplished by someone who is self-less and who has a high degree of self-control. This is why couples who go to church together, pray together regularly, and attend small groups that focus on personal growth generally report higher satisfaction levels in their marriage and their sex lives. The factors that make for a successful intimate relationship are developed in each individual by the presence of the Holy Spirit.

Maybe you've never made the decision to trust Jesus with your eternity. You would like to have eternal life, and you would like to have a greater ability to love your spouse. All you have to do to get started is to express your faith in what Jesus did for you. Here is a suggested prayer for you to follow. Please understand that the words are not magical. This is simply a way for you to log in with faith to the greatest relationship in the world.

> Jesus, I need You in my life. I have been trying to make it on my own, and I realize it isn't enough. If I'm honest, I have to admit that I keep coming up short. Thank You that You died for my mistakes. Please come into my heart, give me eternal life as a gift, and forgive me what I've done wrong. Give me

access now to the new self and begin making me the person
You want me to be.

Steps of Growth

If you just took the first step in a relationship with Jesus, congratulations! You have just made the most important decision of your life. To promote growth in this new relationship, we encourage you to take the following steps:

- Tell someone you trust what you have done. Sharing your decision with another will solidify it in your heart.

- Begin reading the Bible daily. Start in the New Testament book of John. Take a few minutes at roughly the same time each day to read a few verses, and then think about what you read throughout the day.

- Memorize 1 John 5:11-13.

    And this is the testimony: God has given us eternal life, and this life is in his Son. He who has the Son has life; he who does not have the Son of God does not have life. I write these things to you who believe in the name of the Son of God so that you may know that you have eternal life.

- Begin attending a church that teaches directly from the Bible. Ask your friends for a recommendation in your area.

- If your spouse is willing, begin praying together daily. Don't worry about how you sound. Just talk to God like you would your best friend. Share with Him what is important to you and ask Him to guide your daily activities.

It's a New Day

If you want to become more effective at logging in to the life the new nature can give you, try reading this statement out loud everyday for the next seven days.

Jesus, thank You that You made it possible for me to choose to walk in newness of life. I, therefore, choose today to set my mind on the things above, not on the things that are on earth. I realize that I have died to the old nature and my life is hidden with Christ in God. I choose to consider the members of my earthly body as dead to immorality, impurity, passion, evil desire, and greed. I choose instead to put on the new self who is being renewed to a true knowledge according to the image of Christ (Colossians 3:2-10). Fill me with Your power so that I may be kind and tenderhearted to my spouse. Give me the grace to forgive my spouse just as God in Christ also has forgiven me (Ephesians 4:32). Develop in me the self-control that will allow me to say no to my fears as I say yes to you.

Listen to Your Heart

Jim and Susan had been married for eight years when Susan began to feel emptiness in her life. She loved her husband, but he was difficult to live with. He was stubborn and often expressed anger toward her, especially after he had a couple of drinks. He worked hard but consistently brought a bad attitude home.

She didn't want to get divorced, but she didn't think she could keep this up forever. To find some solace, she responded to an invitation from a friend to attend church. She began to cry during the singing time, though she wasn't sure why. As

> Jesus loves you. He wants to give you a new life filled with love and purpose.

the pastor spoke, the words seemed to have been designed just for her. When he said, "If your life is empty and you feel all alone, even though you are surrounded by people, you need to know that Jesus loves you. He wants to give you a new life filled with love and purpose," she squirmed in her seat. She got out of church quickly that day, but she was impressed by the friendliness she observed among the people.

She decided to go back the next week and again felt as if the service had been designed just for her. At the end of the service, the pastor said, "Are you tired of the life you have been able to build on your own? Then today is your day. If you would like to ask Jesus to come into your heart to be your savior and the boss of your life, come forward as we sing. We would love to pray with you and explain how you can know Jesus personally." Susan knew this was for her, so she responded and invited Jesus to live in her heart for the rest of her life.

When she got home, she looked at Jim differently than she ever had. She couldn't explain the change, but she saw Jim as a wounded little boy who was covering up his pain with anger, stubbornness, alcohol, and insults. Compassion took root in her heart, and a patient love began to inspire new thoughts in her head. She continued to attend church and joined a women's Bible study. After about four months, she got the idea that she should begin to pray for Jim. She asked him, "Can I pray for you before you go to bed?"

Surprisingly, he agreed, and she began a routine of scratching his back for a few minutes every night and praying over him. "Dear Jesus, thank you for Jim. Please give him strength for work tomorrow. I so appreciate the way he provides for our family. I know that his shoulder has been hurting so please give him relief from the pain. I also know that he gets angry at times, and he must have some pain inside that is hard to carry. Please take the pain away and help Jim find the pursuits in life he enjoys the most. Amen."

Jim didn't respond for about eight months. Every night, Susan would ask if she could pray for Jim. Every night Jim would say, "If you want to." He never said he liked it. He never said he didn't like it. He simply said, "If you want to." One night, Susan apparently forgot to pray. Jim was in bed, and Susan was on the computer.

Jim came out to find her and asked, "Aren't you going to pray for me before I go to sleep?"

Susan was stunned. She thought Jim didn't care whether she prayed or not, but now she realized that God was at work. With new enthusiasm, she continued to scratch Jim's back and pray for him nightly.

Jim was driving in his car shortly after, flipping through radio stations, when a voice caught his attention, "Have you been stubbornly resisting the one who loves you the most?" He was mesmerized. That was exactly how he was feeling. Susan was being so nice to him, and he was being real hard on her. He was critical of her, careful to point out her faults any time he could. Still, she prayed for him every night. He would stop by the bar on the way home from work because he knew she didn't like it. Still, she prayed for him every night. He would swear at her when he was mad and would call her derogatory names every once in a while. Still, she prayed for him every night.

The radio preacher continued, "The reason you're so hard on people is that you're afraid. You're scared that you won't have freedom to be yourself if you truly love. Well, Jesus created you, and He loves you and wants to give you the power to be the best 'you' possible. All you have to do is ask Him into your life and let Him lead."

It all came together for Jim at that moment. He had been trying to push Susan away because he had been pushing Jesus away. He knew right then that what he really wanted was both of them. He was tired of trying to be somebody and hurting the people he loved the most in the process. He prayed right there in his truck.

> Hi, Jesus, this is Jim. I've been afraid of You because I thought You would take away what I loved. I guess that's not true. I realize today that You love me, and You sent Susan into my life to convince me of that. Would You please forgive me for being so stubborn and critical? Would You also please come into my life and make me the best possible me I can be. Thanks. Amen.

Jim got ready for bed that night and waited for Susan to come pray for him. When she came into the room, Jim surprised her with a different request. "Can I pray for you tonight?" he asked. Susan didn't say a word as Jim began to scratch her back as he quietly prayed, "Hey, Jesus, this is a good woman. Thanks for using her to help me meet You. Please take good care of her and tell her she has done real good. Amen."

The Spirit Decoder

God's Spirit works in connection with God's Word and your heart. Often, something in the Bible will be exactly what you need to gain the access code or password to your mate's heart and move above the line.

Just recently, Bill and I found ourselves off rhythm with one another. I was frustrated by the many tasks still remaining on Bill's to-do list that I thought should have been checked off. In short, I was afraid he would let me down.

I (Bill) was frustrated by what seemed to me to be unrealistic expectations. I was afraid that I would never be able to live up to her demands on me.

There had been an underlying cooling of the temperature of our relationship over a few days, and I (Pam) began to pray that God would show me who needed to change and own the issue. I secretly hoped it would be Bill so I'd get a heartfelt apology. I could then valiantly forgive him, and I wouldn't have to change my to-do list for him!

I often listen to *Walk the Word* music that I've downloaded onto my iPod. That day at the gym I was listening to the *New Testament Experience,* and there, piped into my headphones, was some wonderfully irritating insight.

Ephesians 4:1-3 was dramatically read into my heart: "As a prisoner for the Lord, then, I urge you to live a life worthy of the calling you have received. Be completely humble and gentle; be patient, bearing with one another in love. Make every effort to keep the unity of the Spirit through the bond of peace."

God's Spirit gently asked me, *Have you been humble toward Bill or have you already decided it has to be Bill's fault? Have you been gentle? Patient? Have you been bearing with him and all the pile of responsibilities on his list coming from all different directions? When was the last time you said thank you instead of barking out orders or e-mailing requests for action? Pam, have you made every effort to bless Bill? Every effort to encourage Bill? Every effort to lower his stress? Every effort to meet his emotional needs? You are a relationship specialist, so you know better. Have you really been living worthy of your calling? Pam, pause for a moment, right here in this gym, and pray. Ask Me what you can do for Bill that will help him feel My love, My plan, My hope. The way to your hope, Pam, is to meet Bill's needs right now rather than have him meet yours.*

Overall, Bill and I try to be kind to one another in the workplace, and we both try to go "over the top" in our encouragement to each other. We have high respect for the baggage that is still being redeemed from our pasts, and we do not want to put more pressure than necessary on each other. However, the pressure of a looming deadline had taken the place of our positive interactions.

Fortunately, I knew this part of our marriage code and decided to put into action the message that had been spoken into my heart. I called Bill up, took him to his favorite coffeehouse, and apologized. I told him the story of how God's Spirit had instructed me, and then I listed off all the traits of his I appreciated but had been taking for granted. Emotional reconnection happened almost instantaneously. Physical connection, or red-hot monogamy as we like to call it, happened that night behind our bedroom door.

Carry the decoder, the Bible, under your arm. Listen to the decoding engineer, the Spirit, in your heart, and you'll see, day after day, moment after moment, that your relationship will move, then stay "above the line." Enjoy life over the line!

 **UNLOCKING THE CODE:**

Dinner and Dialogue for a Heart-to-Heart Connection

Go on a date and talk about what you and your mate can do to gain a closer walk with the "Ultimate Decoder," God and His Spirit. Take a step closer to a love that is lived "above the line." Pray together and invite God's Spirit to reign in your love. Then take a step over the line together and each pray:

> *Husband's prayer:* Lord, You know my desire to succeed. Please help me view success from Your vantage point. Give me the

ability to succeed in life through Your power, not my own. Most importantly, help me succeed with my wife and give me ideas and the wisdom to help her feel more secure in life and love.

Wife's prayer: Lord, You know my desire to feel secure. Please help me view You as my safety net, my shield, my protector and provider. As I rest in my security in You, help me feel secure in my husband's love. Give me the ability to succeed in life through Your power not my own. Most importantly, help me function from a place of security so I can be a better helpmate to my husband and his success.

■ ■ ■

The local news station was interviewing an 80-year-old lady who had just gotten married for the fourth time because she had outlived her previous three husbands. The interviewer asked her about her life, about what it felt like to be marrying again at 80, and then about her new husband's occupation.

"He's a funeral director," she answered.

"That's interesting," the newsman said. He then asked her if she wouldn't mind telling him a little about her first three husbands and what they did for a living.

She paused for a few moments, needing time to reflect on all those years. Then a smile came to her face as she recounted that she'd first married a banker when she was in her early thirties, then a circus ringmaster when in her forties, later on a preacher when in her sixties, and now in her eighties, a funeral director.

The interviewer looked at her, quite astonished, and asked why she had married four men with such diverse careers.

She smiled and said, "I married one for the money, two for the show, three to get ready, and four to go."

ABOVE THE LINE

At Sunday school they were teaching how God created every-thing, including human beings. Little Johnny seemed especially intrigued when the teacher told him how Eve was created out of one of Adam's ribs. Later in the week, his mother noticed him lying down as though he were ill.

"Johnny, what's the matter?" she said.

Johnny responded, "I have pain in my side. I think I'm going to have a wife."

Notes

1. http://monster-island.org/tinashumor/humor/moretechsupp.html

2. "Psychologists at the University of Seattle's 'Love Lab' Are Using Science to Uncover the Real Reason Why Marriages Succeed or Fail," *New Age Journal*, September/October 1994 (found at http://www.holysmoke.org/fem/fem0430.htm)

3. "So far as inherited diseases and childhood infections are concerned, the answer appears to lie in the twenty-third pair of chromosomes, where the presence or absence of a Y chromosome determines a person's sex. Unlike the Y chromosome, which carries little if any genetic information and whose only positive effect is to lead to maleness, the larger X chromosome contains a lot of information about how we develop. For example, its instructions can affect the colour of the eyes, composition of the blood, and skin texture. Occasionally the X chromosome is flawed: it may contain too little information for a certain part of the body to develop properly, or perhaps the message is jumbled up. When this happens, all is lost for the male. He has only one X, and to the extent that it is at fault, some aspect of his development must necessarily be faulty. His body has no choice but to obey the faulty instructions on his single X chromosome, and as a result he is born with an abnormality. But females have a second X, carrying duplicate information, and so long as this is not damaged in the same way, it will be able to supply the relevant information in the correct form, and thus cancel out the effects of the defective chromosome." John Nicholson, *Men and Women: How Different Are They?* (Walton Street, Oxford: Oxford University Press, 1984), 47-48.

4. For more information on gender differences, see Bill and Pam Farrel, *Men Are Like Waffles, Women Are Like Spaghetti* (Eugene, OR: Harvest House Publishers, 2001), 11-14.

5. For more information, see Gary D. Chapman, *The Five Love Languages* (Chicago, IL: Northfield Publishing, 1992, 1995).

6. Kristin Cobb, "His-and-Her Hunger Pangs: Gender Affects the Brain's Response to Food," *Science News*, 6 July 2002.

7. For details of how we worked through the forgiveness process, see our book, *Love, Honor and Forgive* (Downers Grove, IL: InterVarsity Press, 2000).

8. Thomas Crook, *The Natural Love Drug*, WebMD feature from *Prevention*, http://www.webmd.com/sex-relationships/features/the-natural-love-drug.

9. John Gottman, *Why Marriages Succeed or Fail: And How You Can Make Yours Last* (New York: Fireside, 1994, 1995), 29, 57.

10. Personal story written by Dawn Wilson.

11. Karen Peterson, *USA Today*, 1 April 1999, "Friendship Makes Marriages a Success," quoting John Gottman, a researcher from the University of Washington.

12. Questions adapted from John Gottman, and Nan Silver, *The Seven Principles for Making Marriage Work* (New York: Three Rivers Press, 1999), 50.

13. http://www.007b.com/breastfeeding_sexual.php

14. Brandon O'Brian, *Out of Ur*, "The Life You've Always Wanted (in Bed)," http://blog.christiani tytoday.com/outofur/archives/2008/07/the_life_youve.html.

15. http://ky.essortment.com/sleepdeprivatio_rloc.htm.

16. http://www.news-medical.net/?id=516.

17. http://www.sleepfoundation.org/site/c.huIXKjM0IxF/b.2419253/k.7989/Sleep_Facts_and_Stats. htm.

18. http://www.robinsfyi.com/food/coffeelite.htm.

19. http://www.forbes.com/home/2006/08/23/Marriage-Careers-Divorce_cx_mn_land.html.

20. http://www.askmen.com/fashion/austin_60/92_fashion_style.html.

21. http://www.mensrights.com.au/page15n.htm.

22. http://www.lotsofjokes.com/cat_314.htm.

23. For more information on nonverbal communication, see http://www.helpguide.org/mental/ EQ6_nonverbal_communication.htm and http://stephan.dahl.at/nonverbal/non-verbal_com munication.html.

24. http://www.romancestuck.com/jokes/marriage-jokes.htm.

25. Emily Nussbaum, "Inside the Love Lab: A Research Psychologist Goes Pop," *Lingua Franca*, March 2000.

26. Jane R. Rosen-Grandon, Jane E. Myers, and John A. Hattie, "The Relationship Between Marital Characteristics, Marital Interaction Processes, and Marital Satisfaction," *Journal of Counseling and Development*, 1 January 2004.

■ ■ ■

For more resources to enhance your relationships
and build marriages or to connect with Bill and Pam Farrel
for a speaking engagement, contact

Farrel Communications
Masterful Living Ministries
3755 Avocado Boulevard, #414
La Mesa, CA 91941

800-810-4449

info@farrelcommunications.com

www.farrelcommunications.com

For help with marriage issues in midlife, visit
www.seasonedsisters.com

■ ■ ■

Other Great Harvest House Books
by Bill and Pam Farrel

MEN ARE LIKE WAFFLES—
WOMEN ARE LIKE SPAGHETTI
Bill and Pam Farrel

Bill and Pam explain why a man is like a waffle (each element of his life is in a separate box), why a woman is like spaghetti (everything in her life touches everything else), and what these differences mean. Then they show readers how to achieve more satisfying relationships. Biblical insights, sound research, humorous anecdotes, and real-life stories make this guide entertaining and practical. Readers will feast on enticing insights that include:

- letting gender differences work for them
- achieving fulfillment in romantic relationships
- coordinating parenting so kids receive good, consistent care

Much of the material in this rewarding book will also improve interactions with family, friends, and coworkers.

MEN ARE LIKE WAFFLES—
WOMEN ARE LIKE SPAGHETTI STUDY GUIDE
Bill and Pam Farrel

This easy-to-use study guide will take you to a new level in your appreciation of the differences and special delights of your mate. Designed to address the important issues of a happy marriage, this guide will

- make planning time with each other fun and exciting
- help you and your mate coordinate parenting so your kids get the best
- bring out the best you have to give in sex, romance, and communication

This guide is great for leading couples in biblically based discussions or for couples to use on their own to create their own marriage retreat.

SINGLE MEN ARE LIKE WAFFLES—
SINGLE WOMEN ARE LIKE SPAGHETTI
Bill and Pam Farrel

Do you wonder how to relate to the opposite sex? Do you want to build a stronger relationship with your girlfriend or boyfriend? In this great book, Bill and Pam help "waffles" and "spaghettis" explore:

- how to meet other singles
- the advantages and disadvantages of being male and female
- what to do if you're single again with kids

Discover how a relationship with God can fulfill your key needs. A discussion guide is included for small group or personal use.

RED-HOT MONOGAMY:
MAKING YOUR MARRIAGE SIZZLE
Bill and Pam Farrel

Did you know that the best sexual experiences are enjoyed by married couples? Bill and Pam reveal how you can add spark and sizzle to your love life. You'll discover how

- God specifically designed you to give and receive pleasure from your mate
- a little skill turns marriage into red-hot monogamy
- sex works best emotionally, physically, and physiologically

Along with ways to create intimacy when you're just too tired and how to avoid the "pleasure thieves," this book offers hundreds more ideas to inspire romance and passion in every aspect of your lives together.

THE 10 BEST DECISIONS A WOMAN CAN MAKE
Pam Farrel

Pam encourages you to exchange the fleeting standards of the world for the steadfast truths found in a growing, fruitful relationship with God. You'll discover the joy of finding your place in God's plan as you

- realize how precious you are to the Lord
- find a positive place to direct your creativity, energy, and enthusiasm
- gain confidence regarding the value of your time and efforts

Pam's warm, motivating message will touch your heart as you seek all God has for you.

WOMAN OF CONFIDENCE
Pam Farrel

Pam helps you discover that nothing is more vital to your self-confidence than your confidence in God. Your ability to achieve, to move through life with courage and boldness, rests on the character, power, and strength of God. Develop the confidence you need to walk into your hopes, dreams, and aspirations.

Great for your women's group or for personal encouragement.

FANTASTIC AFTER FORTY!
The Savvy Woman's Guide to Her Best Season of Life
Pam Farrel

Pam offers words of encouragement, challenge, and humor for women between the ages of 40 and 60. Her 40 ways to forge a fulfilling future include:

- Take control of health and maximize energy
- Embrace God's power and truth and experience renewal
- Discover your uniqueness to live your purpose

Designed for personal or group study, this empowering read is just the beginning of Pam's conversation with baby-boomer women who desire life-enhancing resources and who want to pass them along to other women.